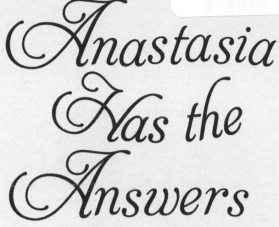

Anastasia
Has the
Answers

Books by Lois Lowry

Anastasia Krupnik

Anastasia Again!

Anastasia at Your Service

Anastasia Off Her Rocker

Anastasia on Her Own

Anastasia Has the Answers

Anastasia at this Address

Anastasia's Chosen Career

Anastasia, Absolutely

A Summer to Die

Find a Stranger, Say Goodbye

Autumn Street

Taking Care of Terrific

Us and Uncle Fraud

The One Hundredth Thing About Caroline

Switcharound

Anastasia Has the Answers

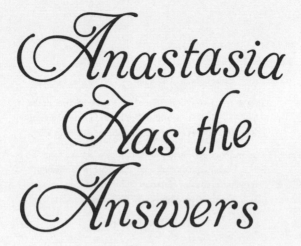

Lois Lowry

Houghton Mifflin Harcourt
Boston   New York

For information about permission to reproduce selections from this book,
write to trade.permissions@hmhco.com or to Permissions,
Houghton Mifflin Harcourt Publishing Company,
3 Park Avenue, 19th Floor, New York, New York 10016.

www.hmhco.com

The text of this book is set in Adobe Garamond Pro

The Library of Congress has cataloged the hardcover edition as follows:
Lowry, Lois.
Anastasia has the answers.
Summary: Anastasia continues the perilous process of growing up as her thirteenth
year involves her in conquering the art of rope climbing, playing Cupid for a
recently widowed uncle, and surviving a crush on her gym teacher.
[1. Humorous stories.] I. Title.
PZ7.L9673Amg 1986   86-330

ISBN: 978-0-395-41795-9 hardcover
ISBN: 978-0-544-54033-0 paperback

Manufactured in the United States
DOC 10 9 8 7 6 5 4 3 2
4500624494

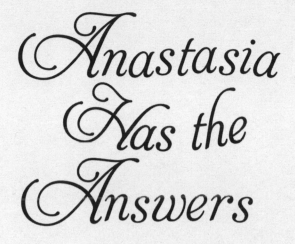

Anastasia
Has the
Answers

"I would sort of like to go," Anastasia said, "because I've never been on an airplane in my life and I would sort of like to take a plane trip."

"So shall I make three reservations? Have you decided?" Her mother was sitting beside the telephone and she had the yellow pages open to AIRLINES. With her ballpoint pen she drew a circle around a number and reached over to dial.

"Weeeellll," Anastasia said indecisively, "I think I might be scared of flying. Maybe I ought to start my flying career with a real short flight, just to Nantucket or something, instead of all the way to California."

Mrs. Krupnik sighed. "All right then. If that's how

you feel, maybe you're correct. I'll make two reservations, for Dad and me."

Anastasia began to chew on a strand of hair. "On the other hand—" she said, with hair in her mouth.

"On the other hand *what?*"

"I've never been to California in my life. This may be my only chance. And since I've decided to become a journalist, I should be open to new experiences."

"I guarantee you will have other opportunities to go to California. However, if you want to go tomorrow, you have to say so right now, Anastasia."

"I have an English test tomorrow, on *Johnny Tremain*. So I should stay here."

"Look at me," her mother announced. "Watch my finger closely. I'm dialing the phone. Make up your mind." She pressed several of the buttons on the telephone.

"But I hated *Johnny Tremain*," Anastasia went on. "I'll probably flunk the test. So maybe I should go."

"It's ringing," her mother announced. "Decide."

"But of course it's not going to be a *fun* trip or anything. No time to go to Disneyland. You did say that, didn't you, Mom—no Disneyland, no movie stars' houses or anything?"

Her mother nodded. She was listening intently to the voice on the telephone. Finally she looked up in disgust. "Rats," she said. "I'm on hold. A recording told me that all their personnel are busy at the moment. Do you believe that? I don't. I think they're all drinking coffee."

She held the receiver out, and Anastasia listened for a moment to the music playing. "Yeah," she said. "They're probably all hanging out together, drinking coffee. But it does give me another minute to decide. If I *go,* all my friends will be jealous, which would be nice. But probably I should stay, to help take care of Sam."

"Sam will be fine. It's only two days, and Mrs. Stein loves taking care of him."

"Realistically, Mom, what do you think the chances are of a movie scout noticing me during two days in Los Angeles?"

"Realistically? Zero."

Anastasia scowled. "You could have said something more supportive, Mom," she said.

"I'm being honest, and honesty is supportive. Here are the facts, Anastasia: It will be an exhausting trip, out to Los Angeles and back for only two days. It will not be fun—no Disneyland or tours of movie studios. On the other hand, Dad and I would be happy to have you come with us, and your Uncle George would appreciate it, I know, and— Yes? Hello?" She turned back to the telephone. Someone had finally answered.

Anastasia shook her head hard. "No," she said. "I don't want to go."

"One moment, please," her mother said into the phone. She covered the receiver with one hand and turned to Anastasia. "You're sure? You don't want to come?"

"Positive. I'll stay here."

Mrs. Krupnik spoke again into the telephone. "I'd like two reservations, please, from Boston to Los Angeles tomorrow morning, returning on Thursday. Myron and Katherine Krupnik."

Anastasia got up from her chair and wandered over to the refrigerator. She took out a piece of leftover chicken, two pickles, some grapes, and a chunk of cheese; carefully she piled it all on a plate and took it to the kitchen table. She began to eat, even though it would be dinnertime in an hour. She was starving.

Decision-making was so hunger-producing when you were thirteen.

Later in the evening, after Sam was in bed, Anastasia wandered into her parents' bedroom to watch them pack for the trip.

"Would you guys like to know the real reason I decided not to go with you?" she asked.

Her father was polishing a pair of shoes that he planned to pack. Her mother was putting some jewelry into a small traveling case. They both looked over to where Anastasia was standing in the doorway, eating an apple.

"Sure," her father said.

"I was scared," Anastasia confessed.

"Of flying?" her mother asked. "You mentioned that. I was surprised. You're not usually scared of new experiences."

"No," Anastasia said, "not of flying. I'd really like to go someplace in an airplane. The new experience I'm scared of is—yuck, I even hate the word—*funerals*."

"But, Anastasia," her mother said, "you went to

your grandmother's funeral when you were only ten years old. I remember that you behaved beautifully and that afterward you said you had *liked* being there, that it was a nice chance to hear people talk about your grandmother and their memories of her."

Anastasia bit into her apple again. "True," she said, chewing. "But you can see what the difference is. The *age* thing, for one."

"Well, you were ten then, and you're thirteen now. You're more mature—that should make it even easier," her mother said.

"I mean the age of the, ah, the deceased person," Anastasia pointed out.

Dr. Krupnik nodded. "I can understand that. Your grandmother was in her nineties, and your Aunt Rose—well, let me see. Katherine, how old was Rose?"

Mrs. Krupnik wrinkled her forehead, thinking. "Fifty-five, maybe?" she said, finally.

"See?" said Anastasia. "That's *old,* but still, it's not like ninety-two. And also, there's the other thing."

Her parents looked at her.

"Other thing?" her mother asked.

Anastasia cringed. "I don't quite know how to say it. Cause of Death."

Her parents both nodded. They looked very sad.

"Grandmother just died in her sleep, remember? And that seemed okay, because she was so old and tired, anyway. But Aunt Rose—well, I'm sorry, Dad, because I know she was your brother's wife and all, and I guess she was an okay lady, even though I don't really remember her because I hadn't seen her since I was little, but I have to tell you that I am really grossed out by her Cause of Death."

"Food poisoning? It's tragic," her father said, "but I wouldn't call it gross."

"That other word. I heard you say it to Uncle George on the phone."

"Salmonella."

"YUCK!"

"Why yuck? It's the medical term for a particular kind of food poisoning."

Anastasia made a face. "It sounds like someone's name. A mobster. A hit man. My Aunt Rose was killed by Sal Monella. It sounds like something a journalist should write about. By the way, do you know that when you write a newspaper story you should answer the questions 'who, what, when, where, and why' right in the very first paragraph?"

Dr. Krupnik sighed and put his newly polished shoes into the suitcase. "Well, here's the who, what, when, where, and why," he said. "Your Aunt Rose was unfortunately killed last night by one of the finest restaurants in Los Angeles, where she made the mistake of ordering some food that had not been properly stored and refrigerated. And as a result, incidentally, your Uncle George will no doubt collect a fortune in a legal settlement."

"No kidding? Uncle George will be *rich?*"

"I'm quite sure he would much prefer to have Rose back," Mrs. Krupnik said. "They never had a lot of money, but they were very happily married." She put a blouse into the suitcase, and sighed. "Poor George. This *is* going to be a sad, sad funeral, Myron," she said. "Anastasia's right. I don't blame her for not wanting to go."

"Since I'm not going, I should be reading *Johnny Tremain* again," Anastasia confessed gloomily. "I know I'll flunk the test."

"No, you won't," her father reassured her. "You always do well in English."

Anastasia sat down in the middle of her parents' king-sized bed and curled her legs up under her. She tossed her apple core into the wastebasket. "I wish they'd assign *Gone with the Wind* in seventh-grade English," she said.

Her mother looked over from where she was folding a nightgown. "They couldn't," she said. "It's too risqué."

"*Mom,*" Anastasia said, "there isn't a single sex scene in *Gone with the Wind*. And only one 'damn.' Remember when Rhett Butler says to Scarlett—"

"'Frankly, my dear, I don't give a damn,'" Mrs. Krupnik said in a deep voice along with Anastasia, and they both laughed.

Dr. Krupnik made a face. "It's terrible literature," he said.

"But it's so romantic, Dad. I love romance. I wish someone would say to me, in a deep voice: 'Frankly, my dear, I don't give a damn.' Someone rich and handsome, with a mustache, like Clark Gable."

Anastasia pulled her long hair up into a pile on

top of her head. She rose to her knees so that she could see herself in the mirror on the opposite wall. With one hand she held her hair in place, and with the other she pulled the neck of her sweatshirt down over one shoulder. "Do you think I have a swanlike neck, Mom?" she asked.

Her mother glanced over at Anastasia's neck. "Long and skinny, yes," she said. She went to the closet. "Myron," she asked, "what ties do you want to take? You'll need something dark and somber, for the services."

Anastasia pulled her sweatshirt tight around her and looked sideways toward the mirror, to see her body in profile. "Would you call me voluptuous?" she asked.

"No," said her father. "Thank goodness. I don't want a voluptuous thirteen-year-old daughter. You can be voluptuous when you're twenty-seven, not before."

Anastasia flopped back down on the bed and sighed. "Well," she said, "I don't know any rich, handsome men with mustaches anyway. I just know obnoxious seventh-grade boys. None of them even shave yet."

Her mother snapped the suitcase closed. "There," she said. "All set. Anastasia, when you get home from school tomorrow, Mrs. Stein will be here, with Sam. Give her a hand with things, would you? And we'll be back late Thursday afternoon."

"It's ten o'clock, Anastasia," said her father. "You ought to be getting to bed."

Anastasia disentangled her legs and stood up. She kissed her father and her mother and went to the hall.

"Don't be dismayed if you notice lights in my room all night long," she called back to them. "I will probably be reading *Johnny Tremain* three or four times, because I know how important it is to you guys that I get an A in English."

She could hear her father's voice respond as she headed up the stairs to her third-floor bedroom.

"Frankly, my dear," he was calling in a deep voice, "I don't give a—"

Giggling, Anastasia closed her door. She sprawled on her bed and took out the notebook in which she was practicing for a journalism career.

Who What When Where Why

In the early hours of California's coastal dawn, Rose Krupnik, 55, was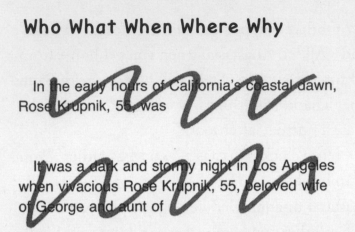

It was a dark and stormy night in Los Angeles when vivacious Rose Krupnik, 55, beloved wife of George and aunt of

Rose Krupnik, wife of Los Angeles businessman George Krupnik (brother of well-known Harvard professor Myron) expired yesterday because of the sinister manipulations of Sal Monella, and brought grief to a Boston household which includes Anastasia Krupnik, 13, aspiring journalist.

two

The test on *Johnny Tremain* was grim. Anastasia hadn't bothered looking at the book again the night before. Now, in school, she answered the questions as well as she could —but she knew it wasn't very well.

When she had finished, she leaned back in her seat and stared out the window of the classroom. Maybe, she thought, instead of a journalist, she should be an English teacher when she grew up. Probably there was a rule that seventh graders had to read a historical novel—that was why they assigned *Johnny Tremain* every year. But she, when she became an English teacher, would definitely assign *Gone with the Wind* in seventh grade.

She began to compose a test on *Gone with the*

Wind. The short-answer questions were easy: the names of Scarlett's sisters, stuff like that.

Essay questions were tougher. But Anastasia had a good one:

"Scarlett O'Hara seemed to think that Ashley Wilkes was a wimp. Do you agree, or disagree? Give your reasons."

Anastasia sort of agreed. Ashley and Melanie were *both* kind of wimpy. But she wasn't exactly sure why. She tried to think of some reasons. If they had lived in current times, Melanie probably would have worn lace-up shoes. Ashley would have gone to the symphony instead of rock concerts — just like Anastasia's father, who was occasionally pretty wimpy himself, in a lovable sort of way.

"Anastasia?"

She jumped. It was Mr. Rafferty, standing by her desk and reaching for her test paper. Blushing, she handed it to him.

"Sorry," she said. "I finished a while ago, and I was thinking about other stuff."

"The poem you're memorizing for next week, I hope," Mr. Rafferty said.

"No sweat, I know it by heart already. I gotta go, Mr. Rafferty. I can't be late for my next class."

The other kids in the class were already out of their seats and heading for the hall. Hastily Anastasia grabbed her books and followed them. She caught up with her friends Sonya and Meredith on the way to gym.

"Where's Daphne?" Anastasia asked. Daphne Bellingham shared her gym locker, and they always went to gym class together. But lately it had been hard to find Daphne a lot of the time.

Meredith sighed. "She's in the guidance office again. Poor Daph. I wish her problems would go away."

"Yeah, me too," Anastasia agreed. "But it would take a U-Haul van to haul them off, she has so many."

"Well," Sonya said optimistically, "at least she's getting guidance. That's what the guidance counselor is for."

"Mrs. Farnsworth?" Anastasia said cynically. "You really think that Mrs. Farnsworth can do anything for Daphne?"

Meredith and Sonya chuckled. Mrs. Farnsworth

was a wimp for sure. Compared to Mrs. Farnsworth, Melanie in *Gone with the Wind* was a punk-rocker.

And Daphne did have big problems. Her parents had separated and were getting divorced. Her father, the Congregational minister, was staying in the church rectory where the family had lived, and Daphne and her mother had moved to a small apartment. Daphne's mother had started a job as a secretary in a lawyer's office.

"Remember Alice in Wonderland, how she drank from that weird magic bottle and ate that freaky cookie and went from large to small and back again? That's how I feel," Daphne had explained to Anastasia. "Family, no family. House, no house. Money, no money. Surprises every day. I never know when I wake up in the morning what that day's surprise will be."

Anastasia hadn't known what to say. "I'm really sorry" was the best she could do.

Now, as she hurried to gym with her friends, she heard the latest news about Daphne. "Her father has a girlfriend, one of the Sunday school teachers at his church," Meredith explained in a whisper. "And Daphne can't decide whether to be nice to her or not. Daphne likes the lady okay, but of course her mother is sort of inclined to commit a really violent murder, maybe bashing the lady over the head with a Bible stories book."

"And Daphne wants to be supportive of her mother," Sonya went on, "so she doesn't really know what to do."

"Well," Anastasia said dubiously, "I don't know what to suggest. I don't even think I could write a newspaper article about Daphne's family. The whos and whats and whens and wheres and whys are too complicated."

In the gym, Anastasia stood in line with the other girls when Ms. Willoughby blew her whistle. But her shoulders were slumped. She wasn't even thinking about Daphne—who was still in the guidance office and hadn't shown up for gym—anymore. She was thinking about herself, and about the disgusting ropes hanging from the ceiling of the gym.

Everybody else in the class—even Sonya, who was overweight—could climb those ropes. But Anastasia couldn't. She could do everything else okay—all the gymnastics stuff, even the parallel bars and the horse—but she couldn't climb the ropes at all.

And Ms. Willoughby had just announced that they were going to do rope-climbing first, before playing basketball.

I love almost everything about Ms. Willoughby, Anastasia thought. I love her looks (Ms. Willoughby was a tall, lanky black woman); and I love her clothes (in gym class, Ms. Willoughby wore a Vassar sweatshirt and blue denim shorts; out of gym, she wore layers of high-fashion skirts and shirts and sweaters, sometimes several on top of each other—Anastasia thought it the most glamorous way of dressing she had ever seen); and I love her personality (Ms. Willoughby was witty and cheerful and funny); and I love her name (Ms. Wilhelmina Willoughby).

But I hate, hate, HATE her ropes.

Anastasia had even tried to think of a way to sneak into the junior high school gym after dark, when no one was there, and to climb up and take down those six hateful ropes.

But there was no way to do it. She couldn't climb them to begin with—that's why she hated them. So how could she climb up to take them down? Even if she could manage that, *she* would be left way up there perched in the rafters, about a million miles high.

"Six lines, ladies!" Ms. Willoughby blew her whistle and the seventh-grade girls formed six lines. Anastasia stood miserably at the end of one, waiting.

Phweet! The whistle blew, and six girls ran forward and climbed the ropes. Meredith was one, and she moved like a monkey all the way to the top and then back down again in no time.

It must be because her parents are Danish, Anastasia thought gloomily.

Phweet! Six more girls, squealing and giggling, climbed the ropes. Anastasia shuffled forward in line.

Phweet! This time Sonya was one of them. Maybe it's *because* she's plump, Anastasia thought—she would never even have thought the word "fat" about one of her best friends—maybe plump people get better leverage or something.

Phweet! Ms. Willoughby blew the whistle a final time, and Anastasia ran forward dutifully toward her enemy rope. She leaped and grabbed. Her grab was good and high because Anastasia was one of the tallest seventh graders. But her feet just dangled.

She looked to either side. The other girls had all managed to wind their legs around the rope the way they were supposed to. Ms. Willoughby had shown them how at least a billion times. But Anastasia's feet dangled. When she tried to grab the rope with her feet and legs, it began to swing in circles.

"Hold the rope for her, Sonya," Ms. Willoughby called, and Sonya ran forward and held the bottom of Anastasia's rope. But it didn't help. Her feet kicked in space and her arms ached. Around her, the other girls were already starting back down their ropes.

Phweet! Everybody landed on the floor, including Anastasia, who hadn't gone anyplace at all, who had simply dangled in the air. She flushed in embarrassment.

"Get the basketballs, girls!" Ms. Willoughby called. "Anastasia," she said more quietly, "come over here for a minute."

Anastasia walked miserably over to Ms. Willoughby. She was looking at the floor. The other girls were all at the opposite end of the gym, shouting and thumping and bouncing the basketballs.

"I can't do it," Anastasia said in a quavery voice. "I try, but I can't do it."

Ms. Willoughby put her arm around her. "Don't feel bad," she said. "You always try hard. That's the important thing."

"But everybody else can do it," Anastasia said. Embarrassed, she felt a warm tear slide down her cheek.

"One of these days you'll amaze yourself. You'll leap up there and you'll just keep going, all the way to the ceiling."

"You think so?" Anastasia asked, sniffling.

"Sure I do. I *know* so. And you're great at basketball. How about being captain of one team this period?"

"Okay," said Anastasia, beginning to feel a little better.

Ms. Willoughby blew her whistle once again, and Anastasia followed her to the other end of the gym to form the teams.

Sam was playing with Mrs. Stein when Anastasia got home from school. They had built a tower of blocks on the living room floor.

"Hi, Sam," said Anastasia. "Hi, Gertrude."

"Gertrustein and me are playing Bash the Castle," Sam explained. "Watch!" He ran to the other side of the room. "Ready, Gertrustein?" he called.

"Ready!" Gertrude Stein called back, and she

moved out of the way. Anastasia stood back too. She had played Bash the Castle with Sam herself and knew how lethal it could be.

"BASH!" Sam came zooming across the room, and the tower flew in all directions.

"Good one, Sam," said Gertrude. "But time to pick up the blocks now. I'm going to start dinner."

"I invented that game," Anastasia said as she knelt to help pick up the blocks. "I invented that game when I was three years old, just the age Sam is right now. I probably should have patented it and copyrighted it and sold it. I would be a millionaire by now."

"I invented blue milk from food coloring," Sam said. "Could I be a millionaire from that?"

Anastasia shrugged. "I dunno. What about you, Gertrude? Did you ever invent anything?"

Mrs. Stein thought. "Crawling on the floor playing with blocks at the age of seventy-six, as a cure for arthritis. How about that?"

"I don't think it'll sell," Anastasia told her regretfully.

Who What When Where Why

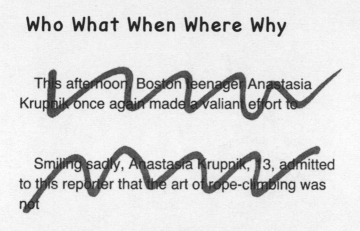

This afternoon, Boston teenager Anastasia Krupnik once again made a valiant effort to

Smiling sadly, Anastasia Krupnik, 13, admitted to this reporter that the art of rope-climbing was not

Anastasia Krupnik, 13, today acknowledged that it was probably her combined poor physical coordination, clumsiness, and lack of fine body tuning that caused her poor showing in this afternoon's rope-climbing event held at the junior high gym. Noted coach Ms. Wilhelmina Willoughby confirmed sadly that Krupnik's bodily agility is not up to normal adolescent standards.

Krupnik also did poorly on an English test, due to lack of preparation and the fact that she did not really read *Johnny Tremain.*

three

$\mathcal{S}$am was asleep, and Anastasia had helped Gertrude with the dishes. Now that Gertrude was ensconced in front of the TV with her favorite program on, Anastasia went to the garage.

It was dark outside, and she turned on the light inside the garage and looked around. There was her parents' battered old car—they had taken a cab to the airport—and there was her father's workbench, with a few scattered tools.

Anastasia grinned. Her father was a terrible handyman. He hit his thumb if he tried to hammer a nail; and if he happened to hit the nail, it bent. He had to squint through his glasses, aiming a screwdriver at the head of a screw, and even then he rarely hit it right.

Once, they had decided that Sam would enjoy a tree house. So Anastasia and her father went to the lumberyard and bought wood.

The boards were still there, leaning against the wall of the garage.

The nails were still there, in a jar.

The hammer was still there, lying on the work-bench.

The book with pictures of wonderful tree houses—the same book that had given them the idea—was still there, very dusty, on a shelf in the garage.

And the tree was still there, in the yard.

But they never could quite figure out how to build the tree house.

She looked around some more. There was the lawn mower, standing in the corner, waiting for sum-mer. There was the snow shovel, standing beside it. There were her mother's gardening tools and a few flowerpots. A plastic gas container. Two gallons of paint—one of these days, her father kept saying, he would paint the trim on the house. Sam's tricycle. Sam's plastic wading pool, deflated. And there — there it was, what Anastasia had been looking for.

A rope.

Anastasia looked up. The cobwebbed ceiling of the garage was nowhere near as high as the ceiling of the school gym. But there were beams up there, strong enough to hold a rope, and if she could figure out how to tie the rope around one of them, she would have a place to practice.

Anastasia was absolutely determined that she would learn to climb a rope and that the day would come when Ms. Wilhelmina Willoughby would look at her with awe and delight instead of pity.

She could *see* that awed and delighted face, brown and cheekboned, poking up out of the neck of a Vassar sweatshirt, in her imagination.

"Anastasia Krupnik!" Ms. Willoughby would say. "I have never in my entire life known a young girl as determined and energetic and dedicated and (well, why not, since it was just a fantasy, anyway?) *gifted* at rope-climbing as you!"

Anastasia picked up the heavy coiled rope and eyed the distance to the ceiling of the garage warily.

Her fantasy continued. A headline in the *Boston Globe*: BOSTON'S GOLD MEDALIST RETURNS FROM OLYMPICS. In smaller letters: ANASTASIA KRUPNIK TAKES GOLD IN ROPE-CLIMBING. A picture: Anastasia smiling graciously, humbly, wearing her gleaming medal. The caption: "I owe my success to my seventh-grade gym teacher, Ms. Wilhelmina Willoughby." And another picture in the center spread after the reader had turned the pages for the rest of the article: Ms. Wilhelmina Willoughby herself, hugging Anastasia warmly and beaming with pride. Caption: "'I always knew this girl could do it! She was my very favorite student!' says former gym teacher, now personal manager for famed athlete Krupnik."

Anastasia threw the rope in the air toward the rafter. It went a few feet into the air and then thumped heavily onto the wooden floor of the garage and lay there in a heap.

Okay. So she couldn't throw a big rope that high. Who could? Nobody but Superman. Time to use the old brains instead of the muscles.

Anastasia draped the rope over her shoulder and climbed onto the hood of her father's car. The metal creaked ominously. Carefully she planted her sneakers and stood up, steadying herself by holding on to the radio antenna.

She was still too far from the beams. She could tell without even throwing the rope this time.

Okay. Onward to plan C. Anastasia sat down on the roof of the car with her legs in front of the windshield. Carefully she skootched backwards and over the luggage rack until she was sitting like the Buddha in the center of the car roof. She could feel it give a little, as if the roof might be starting to sag.

"Crummy Detroit cars," Anastasia muttered. "If we were rich he could buy a BMW and it would withstand anything."

Very slowly she stood up, with her sneakered feet apart for balance and the rope still draped over her shoulder. She measured the distance to the beam with her eyes. It looked manageable.

She uncoiled the big, bristly rope and arranged it in a throwing position. She aimed, watching the rafter high above her. Then she threw.

And it worked! Now she had the rope up there, one end dangling over the beam. Very carefully she maneuvered the end she still held, shaking it gently so that the dangling end moved downward slowly.

There was a shriek. "Anastasia!" The door to the garage burst open. "ANASTASIA! STOP! Suicide is never the answer!"

Anastasia turned toward the door in surprise. The rope fell to the floor.

"*Rats,*" she said, glaring at the tangled heap of rope. "Hi, Daphne."

"Did you walk over?" Anastasia asked when she and Daphne were in the kitchen, sipping hot chocolate with marshmallows. "Does your mom let you wander around like that after dark? Mine wouldn't."

Daphne shrugged. "It's only a few blocks, and I told her I'd be back in an hour. She thought I was going to see my dad, so of course she let me go. She wants me to act as a spy and tell her everything that's going on."

Anastasia felt sad. The house where Daphne used to live—the house where Daphne's father still lived—was right around the corner from the Krupniks'. In the good old days—before the Bellinghams separated—Anastasia and Daphne had run back and forth between the two houses all the time.

"Anyway," Daphne went on, "my mom's so depressed, she hardly notices what I do. She says things like 'Comb your hair' or 'Do your homework' the way all mothers do, but then she never checks to see if I've done it. I could go out with my hair a big disgusting mess and she'd never even—"

"You did, Daph."

"Did what?"

"You went out without combing your hair. It's pretty gross, Daphne," Anastasia said, and giggled.

Daphne felt her hair and laughed. "Yeah. Well, I forgot. My mom used to notice stuff like that, but now that she's so depressed—"

"What about your father? Isn't he depressed too?" Anastasia asked. She remembered that when her parents had a fight, as they did occasionally, *both* of them were pretty miserable until they made up.

But Daphne shook her head. "Not really, because he's dating this woman. She teaches the fourth-grade Sunday school class. I remember she used to make really neat shadow boxes of Bible stories. Daniel in the lion's den and stuff, with little toy lions, all in a shoe box. She borrowed the plastic palm tree from my turtle bowl."

"Is he going to marry her?" Anastasia asked. She tried to imagine what it would be like if her parents married other people. The thought of her father liking a woman who put plastic palm trees into shoe boxes was so foreign that she couldn't even dream up a fantasy about it.

"No, I don't think so. But he says he likes having a woman friend, and it keeps him from being depressed." Daphne finished her hot chocolate and poked her finger into the cup to stab the melted marshmallow.

"That's what your mom needs, then, too. A man friend."

"Hah. She has my Uncle Bill. He comes over for dinner sometimes. And she works for this lawyer, Mr. McDonald. But she's *still* depressed. Honestly, Anastasia, if my mother was in the garage with a rope around the rafters, you *know* she wouldn't be practicing rope-climbing."

"Those aren't friends, though. An uncle, and a guy she works for. She needs a *date*," Anastasia said.

"Who needs a date? Me?" Gertrude Stein shuffled

into the kitchen, wearing her terry-cloth slippers. "I smelled hot chocolate. May I join you?"

"Sure," Anastasia told her. She introduced her to Daphne and poured another cup of hot chocolate. "We were talking about Daphne's mother. She's all depressed because she's getting divorced and she doesn't have a man friend."

"She says she hates all men," Daphne explained. "She says Dad's a sanctimonious creep."

"Is he?" asked Gertrude Stein with interest.

"I don't know." Daphne giggled. "I don't know what 'sanctimonious' means."

"How old is your mother?" Gertrude asked.

"Old," Daphne said. "Thirty-six."

Gertrude wiped her chocolate mustache with a paper napkin. She chuckled. "Well, I can see that it would be a problem, finding a man friend for someone that old."

"You know what?" A thought had just occurred to Anastasia. "Here we are, you and me, Daphne, both of us thirteen, and *we* worry because we don't have boyfriends. And there's your mother, thirty-six, and she's depressed because she thinks she hates all men, which of course isn't true—it's just that she doesn't have a man friend. And here's Gertrude—who's seventy-six. How about you, Gertrude? Does it bother you that you don't have a boyfriend?"

"Maybe she does," Daphne pointed out.

"No, she doesn't," Anastasia said. "There was a guy at the Golden Age Club who asked her out for dinner once, but he turned out to be a jerk. Right, Gertrude?"

Gertrude nodded. "Right. He was a vegetarian, for one thing, and wouldn't let me order steak. I really wanted steak. On top of that, he was boring."

"Well, does it bother you, not having a man friend?" Anastasia asked again. "Or is seventy-six too old for that?"

Gertrude rubbed one hand with the other. Her knuckles were knobby and swollen, from her arthritis. "No," she confessed, almost shyly. "It's not too old. I *do* wish I had a man friend. Someone to do things with occasionally, maybe a movie now and then. I wanted to see *Tootsie,* but not all alone."

"So," Anastasia went on, "you see? All of us worrying, at all these different ages, because we don't have boyfriends. There's probably only one brief fleeting time in your life when you don't have that worry, that time when you're adult but still young, glamorous, and interesting, that time when you're—well, like Ms. Willoughby, for example."

"Our gym teacher?" Daphne asked in surprise. "*That* Ms. Willoughby?"

Anastasia nodded. "The very one. Ms. Wilhelmina Willoughby," she said dreamily.

"That's our gym teacher," Daphne explained to Gertrude Stein. "Anastasia has a crush on her."

"I do *not*," Anastasia said. "But honestly, wouldn't it be neat if only we could all be tall and thin and black, with high cheekbones and a crewcut and beautifully shaped ears, gifted at rope-climbing and owning a layered-look wardrobe? *Then* we wouldn't have to worry about boyfriends. Or man friends. *Then* our phone would be ringing all the time, with rich and handsome men with mustaches calling—"

"But, Anastasia," Daphne interrupted, "Ms. Willoughby doesn't have a man friend. She told me. We had a conference the other day, Ms. Willoughby and me, because I've been skipping gym so much, and we got to talking about life's disappointments. One of Ms. Willoughby's disappointments is that she doesn't have a man friend. She can't figure out where the men are all hiding."

Anastasia looked at Daphne in astonishment. "Ms. Willoughby? Ms. Wilhelmina Willoughby?" she said. "No man friend? You're *sure?*"

Daphne nodded.

"*Rats,*" said Anastasia.

Who What When Where Why

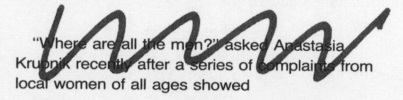

Investigative journalist Anastasia Krupnik, 13, announced yesterday that extensive investigation into the problem of men friends had revealed

"Where are all the men?" asked Anastasia Krupnik recently after a series of complaints from local women of all ages showed

Journalist/athlete Anastasia Krupnik, 13, realized recently that she had been devoting too much time to rope-climbing practice and had not undertaken the more important challenge of locating eligible bachelors for lonely women. Some of these women include neighbor and babysitter Gertrude Stein, 76; legal secretary Caroline Bellingham; and glamorous local gym teacher Ms. Willoughby, on whom reporter Krupnik does not have, and never has had, a crush.

four

$\mathcal{A}$nastasia trudged home from school on Thursday afternoon. It was nice that her parents would be back that evening—she and Mrs. Stein planned to cook a special welcome-home dinner—but that was really the *only* nice thing about the whole day.

She had gotten her *Johnny Tremain* test back, with a C+ on it. Anastasia always got A's in English, so a C+ was a real disappointment. Mr. Rafferty had met with her after school, to discuss it. But there was really nothing to discuss. She hadn't liked *Johnny Tremain,* so she hadn't read it very carefully; and she had been thinking about *Gone with the Wind* during the test.

She had tried to explain that to Mr. Rafferty. "I

think you ought to assign *Gone with the Wind* instead," she suggested. "At least for the girls. Let the boys read *Johnny Tremain*."

Mr. Rafferty looked very startled. He was an ancient, elderly man, probably about sixty, Anastasia thought, with gray hair. The only interesting thing about Mr. Rafferty was that he wore colorless nail polish. Or at least Anastasia *thought* he did. Maybe his fingernails were naturally glistening—but she was pretty certain he wore nail polish. She pictured him at home, at night, preparing English quizzes for the seventh grade—making up sentences with misplaced modifiers—and polishing his nails at the same time, holding them up to see how they looked, blowing on them so they would dry. It seemed very weird.

"*Gone with the Wind*?" Mr. Rafferty said, startled. "But, Anastasia, that book has some, well, some unsuitable—"

"Sex?" she asked. "It doesn't, really. Not explicit."

Mr. Rafferty began to shuffle the papers on his desk nervously, and Anastasia realized that she had made a terrible blunder, saying the word "sex" to someone so old. But now, having said it, she was stuck with completing her explanation.

She tried to describe it very tastefully. "When Rhett carries Scarlett up the stairs," she said, "and into the bedroom, the book doesn't tell a single thing after the door closes. They might have been playing Scrabble in the bedroom, Mr. Rafferty." (Secretly, Anastasia was absolutely certain that Rhett and Scarlett had never played Scrabble in their lives. Ashley and Melanie—*they* played Scrabble, the wimps.)

"Well," Mr. Rafferty said, "ah, I don't—well, what I mean is—"

Anastasia sighed. She knew that Mr. Rafferty would never, ever assign *Gone with the Wind* to the seventh grade.

"Can I take the *Johnny Tremain* test again?" she asked. "I know I can do better if I take it again."

Mr. Rafferty looked relieved, and he scheduled a makeup test for Anastasia and the other students who had done poorly.

"And your poem, Anastasia?" he asked. "You have your poem memorized? We'll start rehearsing on Monday. Don't forget that it's Wednesday when the visitors will be here."

"No problem," she assured him. Mr. Rafferty was such a worrywart.

Walking home, she scowled, realizing that now she would have to read *Johnny Tremain* again. She had wanted to practice rope-climbing tonight, if her father would help her get that rope up in the garage.

That was the other thing about the day: gym again. Rope-climbing again. Failure and humiliation again. Ms. Wilhelmina Willoughby, looking pitying and sympathetic again.

The worst thing in the world, Anastasia decided, was being humiliated while wearing a gym suit. Being humiliated, that was bad. Wearing a gym suit in front of other people, that was terrible. But being humiliated while wearing a royal blue gym suit with gross elasticized legs at the same time—and especially in front of Ms. Wilhelmina Willoughby, the one person Anastasia admired most in the world—well, that was the worst feeling in the world, no question.

Anastasia plodded up the back porch steps, wishing her mother were home from Los Angeles. Anastasia liked Gertrude Stein a lot. But she couldn't really confide in Gertrude about life's problems the way she could with her mom.

And Sam didn't understand about those kinds of

things. Sam often told Anastasia *his* problems, but they were things like "I didn't get to play with the fire truck at nursery school today because Timmy and Jason were hogging it."

Big deal.

Gertrude was busy at the stove when Anastasia entered the house, and the kitchen was filled with a wonderful smell.

"I've started an apple pie for dinner, to welcome your parents back," she announced. "You can help me with the pot roast and the salad."

"I rolled the pie dough," said Sam proudly, looking up from the floor where he had arranged a long line of Matchbox cars. "And I sprinkled the cinnamon. I wanted to do salt and pepper, too, but Gertrustein said No Way."

Anastasia stepped over his line of cars and went to the refrigerator for a snack. "What time do Mom and Dad get home?" she asked.

"Their plane gets in at five, so they should be here by six. They called late this morning, before they left California. And guess what—"

Sam interrupted. "This long line of cars is a funeral," he announced. "They're all driving to the sedentary. *Rrrrrr.*" He crawled across the floor, moving the cars slowly one by one.

"They're *what?*" Anastasia asked. "How do you know about funerals?"

Sam looked up matter-of-factly. "Mom told me. They went to California to a funeral, and they were all going to be in cars and drive in a parade, going to the sedentary."

"Cemetery," Anastasia said.

"Right. That's what I said," Sam replied. "And when they get to the sedentary, the parade stops, like this." He stopped his line of cars in front of the washing machine. "Here. Here's the sedentary. And then they take Aunt Rose —" Sam reached for a small plastic G.I. Joe. "Here's Aunt Rose," he explained. "And they bury her, like a tulip bulb."

He laid the GI Joe on the kitchen floor, covered it with a paper napkin, and smoothed it with his hand. "Goodbye, dead Aunt Rose," Sam said.

"*Sam!*" Anastasia exclaimed. "That's *gross!*"

Sam looked up at her, wide-eyed. "No, it isn't," he said. "Mom said it wasn't. Mom said it was just like trees and flowers and little animals and bugs."

"Well," Anastasia said. Then she couldn't think of anything to add. "Well," she said again.

Sam wrapped G.I. Joe in the napkin and began to gather up all of his cars. "Now," he announced, "I'm going to have another funeral. This one will be in the hall. And the sedentary will be in the study. This time I'm going to bury Aunt Rose under Daddy's desk."

Anastasia and Gertrude watched him as he trotted off with his armload of cars to the hall.

"What were you going to say before Sam interrupted?" Anastasia asked.

Mrs. Stein looked stricken. "I was going to tell you that your parents called to say that they're bringing your Uncle George back home with them for a visit." She stared for a moment down the hall where Sam, on all fours, was arranging his next funeral. "I sure hope," she added, "that Sam gets tired of burying Aunt Rose before they arrive."

Anastasia heard the taxi pull up in front of the house. Sam was upstairs, in the bathtub; she could hear splashing sounds and Mrs. Stein's voice as she talked to him.

Anastasia looked through the front window and saw the driver removing suitcases from the trunk of the cab. She saw her father taking his wallet out of his pocket, and she could see her mother lean over and whisper into her father's ear.

Anastasia knew what she was whispering: "Don't forget to give him a tip, Myron."

She could also see a tall man getting out of the other side of the taxi. Uncle George, obviously.

Quickly Anastasia dashed to the study and made sure that every bit of evidence of Sam's funeral and cemetery was gone. G.I. Joe, alias Aunt Rose, had been returned to the toy box, and all of the Matchbox cars were back on the windowsills in Sam's bedroom, where they usually stayed.

Whew.

"Anastasia? Hi, sweetie, we're home!" It was her mother's voice. Anastasia ran to the front door and greeted both of her parents.

"Dinner smells terrific," her father said as he took off his coat. "It's good to be back. Anastasia, do you remember my brother? This is your Uncle George."

Anastasia turned to shake hands with her uncle,

and she said the words that she had carefully prepared in her head.

"I'm glad you came, Uncle George," she said politely, "and I'm really sorry about Aunt Ro—"

But then she stopped. She stared at him. She could hardly believe it.

"Holy—" Anastasia murmured. Then she caught herself. "I'm really sorry about Aunt Rose," she said again, since the words had trailed off the first time.

"Thank you," Uncle George replied, and smiled at her. He turned to hang up his coat, and Anastasia watched intently. Was it *really* Uncle George? She hadn't seen him since she was two, and she couldn't remember that. Had her parents maybe played a trick? They had had that conversation about Rhett Butler just the other night.

Had they brought Rhett Butler home to meet her?

Well, that was a stupid thought, Anastasia realized. Rhett Butler was a fictional character.

But had they—maybe—brought *Clark Gable* home from California?

That was even more stupid. Clark Gable had been dead for years.

It *was* Uncle George. It had to be. But he looked exactly like Clark Gable.

He's tall, thought Anastasia.

He's handsome.

He has a mustache.

He's — Anastasia remembered her parents saying this — *rich*.

And he is — well, maybe it was gross even to think this, since it was so recent that Sal Monella had done away with Aunt Rose, but let's face it, Anastasia thought; let's be honest — Uncle George is a bachelor.

And Anastasia knew a couple of women who would be thrilled to meet him.

Who What When Where Why

~~Recently widowed, handsome and rich businessman George Krupnik today swept the Boston suburbs off their feet when~~

~~Wealthy mustached George Krupnik, California bachelor and Clark Gable look-alike, was taken firmly in hand by his attractive young niece Anastasia today during~~

Arriving today from the West Coast for a visit, handsome bachelor George Krupnik was pleased to find that his attractive and athletic niece Anastasia was prepared to arrange an interesting social life for him during his stay.

five

"A"nastasia," Gertrude Stein whispered at the Krupniks' back door as she buttoned her sweater and prepared to walk across the yard to her own house, "I'm going to make a very noble gesture. I'm going to relinquish any claims I might have."

"Are you *sure?*" Anastasia asked. "Because I really wanted you to have first shot at him. And I could tell at dinner that you liked him."

Gertrude chuckled. "Where's my bag? Oh, there — on the table. Would you hand it to me, Anastasia?" She took the little overnight bag that she'd been using and turned to leave. "I *do* like him," she said. "He's a very charming man. And you're right — he looks exactly like Clark Gable.

"But I'm afraid he's too young for me, Anastasia," she said. "Now, let's see: toothbrush, nightgown, slippers—I think I've got everything. Good night, Anastasia. Tell your mother I'll talk to her tomorrow."

She gave Anastasia a kiss on the cheek and headed down the porch steps and across the lawn toward her own house next door. Anastasia watched her. Gertrude walked very carefully and slowly because of her arthritis and because her eyesight wasn't what it once had been. She was a little stooped, and her hair was gray and wispy. Still, she was one of Anastasia's very favorite people, and Anastasia wanted Gertrude's life to be happier and less lonely.

"Gertrude!" she called in a loud whisper across the yard.

Mrs. Stein stopped and looked back. "What?"

"*Cosmopolitan* magazine had an article about it and they said it was not only okay but sometimes very desirable!" Anastasia called, trying to keep her voice down so that her parents, in the living room with Uncle George, wouldn't hear.

"*What* was okay? I can't quite hear you!" Gertrude cupped one hand behind her ear.

Anastasia ran down the steps and across the lawn.

"Older women and younger men," she explained breathlessly to Gertrude. "*Cosmopolitan* says that sometimes it's the best combination of all, and you shouldn't back off from it out of fear for what people might say. It's *not* always true that the man is just trying to find a substitute mother!"

Gertrude started to laugh. "All right," she said, "I'll remember that. And if I meet a younger man—maybe seventy-three—I certainly won't back off for fear of what people might say. But I don't think your Uncle George is the one, Anastasia. And it's a little too soon, anyway, for George. Give him a little time, Anastasia. Your Aunt Rose has only been gone four days."

"Yeah, you're right," Anastasia said.

"But thank you," Gertrude added, as she turned to go on into her own yard. "Thank you for thinking of me."

Anastasia thought it over as she went back to the kitchen door, and she knew that Gertrude *was* correct. It was too soon. This was Thursday night. She'd give Uncle George a few more days.

>< >< ><

"There! Got it!" Myron Krupnik called. "Pull it tight now!"

Anastasia stood in the door of the garage, with her mother, watching. It was Friday afternoon. Uncle George was up at the top of an extension ladder, one arm wrapped around the ceiling beam, as he tied the thick rope. Below him, on the floor, Anastasia's father was steadying the bottom of the rope and calling directions.

"Are you sure this is going to be safe?" asked Mrs. Krupnik apprehensively. "Don't forget that Sam already fell out of a second-story window once. I don't think I can deal with *another* skull fracture. That rope is awfully high."

"It's not nearly as high as the one in the gym," Anastasia told her. "Anyway, I never get more than two feet off the ground. I don't think you can fracture your skull if you only fall two feet."

"It's good and tight!" Uncle George called from the top of the ladder. He yanked at the rope a few times. "Look at that! It would hold an elephant!"

Sam appeared at the garage door. "An elephant can't climb a rope," he remarked. "Maybe a snake could, or a monkey. But not an elephant."

George laughed and started down the ladder while Anastasia's father held it steady. "Where did you come from, Sam?" he asked. "You should have seen me up there, like an acrobat."

Sam sat down on the floor of the garage and pulled off one sneaker. He tilted it and dumped out some sand. "I was in my sandbox," he explained to his uncle. "I was making a sedentary in my sandbox. Here, look." He reached into the pocket of his over-alls and pulled out G.I. Joe. "This is poor dea—"

Anastasia interrupted hastily. "Thanks, Uncle George. Thanks, Dad. Now I can practice. Maybe I'll get a decent grade in gym if I learn to climb a rope."

"We used to have to climb ropes in gym," Mrs. Krupnik said. "I wonder if I can still . . ."

She put down the flowerpot she was holding, eyed the rope, and leaped upward suddenly. It was the most amazing thing Anastasia had seen in a long time: her mother leaping into the air, grabbing the rope, and dangling there for a moment. Then she wrapped her legs around, caught the rope in her feet—exactly the way Ms. Willoughby demonstrated, *exactly* the way Anastasia couldn't do it—and up she went, all the way to the ceiling.

"The Ascent of Woman," Anastasia's father said. "What a great book title!"

Back down came Katherine Krupnik, and she jumped off the rope, panting. "What do you think?" she asked proudly. "Great athlete here, or what?"

Anastasia didn't say anything. But no one noticed.

"My turn!" her father said. And off he went, and up he went—in about two seconds. He was so tall that he got a head start. Back down, he dropped from the rope, laughing, and took his pipe from his pocket. "It's all this pipe-smoking that keeps me in such great shape," he said. "How about you, George? You're a former U.S. Marine!"

Uncle George took a deep breath, brushed his hands together, measured the rope with his eyes, and jumped and grabbed. In a flash he was up at the ceiling and back down.

Anastasia still hadn't said anything.

"Now me!" called Sam. He put his G.I. Joe on the floor and held up his hands. "Now me!"

Mrs. Krupnik picked Sam up and held him so that he could grab the rope.

Okay, thought Anastasia. This is it. First my nonathletic thirty-eight-year-old mother climbs the rope. Then my nonathletic, slightly overweight, nicotine-addicted forty-eight-year-old father climbs the rope. Then my grief-stricken fifty-something-year-old uncle climbs the rope. If my three-year-old brother climbs that rope, I will have to leave home. I'll change my name and go to work in a leper colony somewhere and never return.

But Sam just dangled for a moment and then yelled "Help!" His mother lifted him back down.

Whew.

Later, when they had all gone off to do other things, Anastasia made certain that the garage door was closed so that no one would see. And then she tried.

And tried.

And tried.

"Sometimes I wish Sam would just disappear," Anastasia said grouchily to her mother that night. "Sometimes I wish Sam had never been born."

They were doing the dishes together after dinner. "Well," her mother responded cheerfully, "I can understand that. He's a pain in the neck sometimes."

Rats. Anastasia attacked a freshly washed pot angrily with the dishtowel. Her mother was supposed to *argue* with her. Then *she* could say what a pain in the neck Sam was. If her mother agreed right off, then there wasn't any argument, and what was the point of—

"You know what?" her mother said. "George is ten years older than your dad, the same as you're ten years older than Sam. On the plane, coming back from California, they got to talking about old times. And George said pretty much the exact same thing. He thought your dad was a pain in the neck when he was little. He wished he had never been born."

"No kidding?" Anastasia walked to the pantry to put the pot away. "I can't imagine Dad being a pain in the neck, not even when he was little."

Her mother was laughing. "George said, 'Myron, you were such a pompous little showoff.' Apparently your dad was always trying to get attention. But no wonder. You know, he was the youngest of five boys. He probably would have gotten lost in the crowd if he hadn't been a pompous little showoff!"

"Sam's sort of a showoff, too, and he doesn't even have an excuse. He's the only boy. He gets plenty of attention."

Mrs. Krupnik put the last dish away and sat down at the kitchen table. "Are you feeling as if you're not getting enough attention, Anastasia? It has been kind of hectic around here, with Rose's death . . ."

Anastasia pulled out a chair and sat down beside her mother. "No, it's not that. It's that dumb rope. I hate it that I can't climb that rope. When you climbed it, Mom, I was so jealous of you. And I feel that way about every single girl in my gym class, even my best friends."

Mrs. Krupnik reached over and stroked Anastasia's hair. "I think the practicing will do it. I bet you'll be out there some afternoon in the garage and all of a sudden, when you least expect it, ZOOM! There you'll be, up at the top of the rope, amazed at yourself."

Anastasia grinned. "That's what Ms. Willoughby said."

"Who's Ms. Willoughby? Your gym teacher?"

"Yeah." Anastasia felt very shy, even in front of her own mother, who had known her ever since she was born. She wanted to tell her about something, but she felt too shy.

Suddenly she decided that maybe the dishes in

the pantry needed rearranging, so she went to the pantry and began to move them around. She moved the cups from one shelf to another; then she unstacked the plates and restacked them in a different place.

"Mom," she called, from the pantry, "I know this girl at school, and guess what? This is really weird—"

"What? I can't hear you. Why are you clanking all the dishes?"

Anastasia leaned around the doorway. "I know this girl at school," she said. "She's just my age, thirteen?"

"Yes? What about her? Is it someone I know?"

Anastasia's head disappeared. "No," she called. "You don't know her. You never met her. You don't even know her name." Quickly she moved two plates off their stack and put a soup bowl in their place.

"Oh. Well, what about her? Did you want to tell me something about her?"

Anastasia poked her head out again. "It's really *sick*. This girl, who you don't even know her name? She, ah, she has a crush on a teacher." She ducked back into the pantry and rearranged a sugar bowl and a teacup.

"Why is that sick? Lots of your father's students have crushes on him. I think that's fairly typical."

"It's a *woman* teacher!" Anastasia wailed. "Isn't that *gross?*"

"Oh," Mrs. Krupnik said. "I see." She got up from the table and came to the pantry. Anastasia was standing with her back turned and her head down, but she could hear her mother coming. Her mother put her arms around her.

"It isn't gross at all," she said softly. "You can tell your friend that it isn't gross at all. And I'm an authority on that."

"You are?" Anastasia lifted her head a little. "How come?"

"Well, because when I was your age—and the age of this girl you know—thirteen, I had a crush on my piano teacher. A woman. Miss Hermione Fitzpatrick."

"Hermione?"

"Sorry about the name. But I adored her despite it. She was young and she was beautiful and she was a good musician, and—well, what can I say? I loved her. I even had fantasies about living with her after I grew up."

"What happened?"

Her mother shrugged. "Nothing. I got older. I got bored with piano lessons. Hermione Fitzpatrick married an oboe player. I haven't even thought of her for years and years."

"So it didn't have any long-lasting bad effect on you, or anything?"

"Anastasia," her mother said dramatically, "take a look at me." She walked across the kitchen, stood in the center, and posed there, like a model. "Did I turn out okay, or not?"

Anastasia looked. Her mother was wearing jeans with paint smeared on one knee. There were sneakers on her feet, and one yellow sock and one white sock. She was wearing a sweatshirt that said GOD ISN'T DEAD, SHE'S COOKING DINNER across the front. Her hair was tied up in two ponytails, one on each side of her head, both of them a little crooked.

"Yeah," Anastasia conceded. "You turned out okay."

"So. There's your answer."

"So you think that this girl I know, she might get over it? And it doesn't mean that she's weird or anything?" Anastasia came out of the pantry.

"She's not weird at all. What it *does* mean is that she's very normal, very sensitive, very capable of loving. I think I would probably like her a whole lot."

"If you knew her," Anastasia said quickly.

"Yes, of course. If I knew her. Now, are you through rearranging dishes? Would you consider coming into the living room and maybe watching a movie on TV with Dad and Uncle George and me?"

"Yeah, okay, in a minute. Or maybe five minutes. Save me a place on the couch." Anastasia headed for the back door.

"Where are you going? It's dark out," her mother said in surprise.

"To the garage. I'm just going to try the rope one more time," said Anastasia.

Who What When Where Why

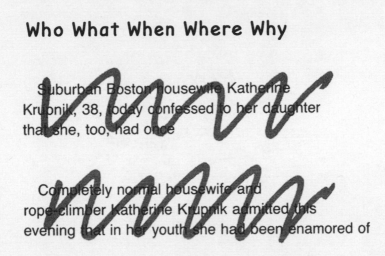

Suburban Boston housewife Katherine Krupnik, 38, today confessed to her daughter that she, too, had once

Completely normal housewife and rope-climber Katherine Krupnik admitted this evening that in her youth she had been enamored of

Boston adolescent Anastasia Krupnik, 13, realized on a recent evening that her extreme affection for her gym teacher was not, after all, symptomatic of serious psychological problems. "What a relief," Krupnik said, after admitting that she had been concerned.

six

Anastasia groaned when she woke up on Saturday morning and looked out the window. The weather was terrible. The big trees in the yard were blowing in the wind, and heavy rain was falling in sheets, splattering her window. There were already deep puddles in the driveway.

Rats.

Anastasia had planned to go over to Daphne's to see the new apartment where Daphne was living with her mother. But it was raining so hard that she couldn't possibly walk or ride her bike.

"Frank," she asked, peering over into the bowl where her goldfish was swimming in circles, "how do you stand being wet all the time?"

Frank Goldfish swirled and twitched his tail. He smiled and said something, his lips moving silently against the side of the bowl.

"I know," Anastasia said, and sighed. "For you, wetness is normal. Here—eat your breakfast." She tapped the fish food box lightly over the bowl, and Frank came up to the surface greedily. "Don't *gobble*," Anastasia scolded him, but he paid no attention.

She dressed in a pair of jeans that she always saved for Saturdays because her mother said they were too disgusting to wear to school, a turtleneck sweater (because her mother had said her neck was long and skinny—which was true—and she was testing various ways to disguise that), and her hiking boots with red laces. Then she brushed her hair briefly.

Anastasia frequently made resolutions to brush her hair a hundred strokes in the morning and a hundred strokes at night. But never once had she actually done it. A hundred strokes was a *lot*.

It was similar, she thought, to the resolution her father was always making about his pipe. "I'm not going to light this pipe again," he would say after supper, "until midmorning tomorrow."

But two hours later he would casually pick up his

pipe again and begin filling it with tobacco. Anastasia and her mother would stare at him meaningfully. Anastasia would hum "Smoke Gets in Your Eyes."

"Well," Dr. Krupnik would say defensively, "until midmorning tomorrow is a *long time*."

It was the same with hair-brushing, Anastasia thought, and put the brush down after stroke fourteen. Her arm got tired. Probably overuse wasn't good for the brush, either.

She put on her glasses, thought briefly about making her bed, decided not to, and left her bedroom. She thumped down the stairs. Her parents weren't crazy about the noise that her hiking boots made on the stairs, but Anastasia kind of liked it. And it was another Saturday thing, like her torn, grubby jeans.

"*Rrrrrrr,*" said Sam. He was on his hands and knees in the hall, arranging another long line of cars. "Watch out, Anastasia. Don't step on my cars. I'm having a—"

"A parade, right? That's neat, Sam: a lovely parade."

"Nope," Sam said in a loud, cheerful voice. "Another funeral."

"Shhhhh." Anastasia knelt beside her brother and

whispered, "Don't say that so loud. Not while Uncle George is here."

"Why not? Uncle George knows all about funerals, because Aunt Rose just—"

"SHHHHHHH!"

Sam pointed to a small metal dump truck. G.I. Joe was lying stiffly in the back of it, his glazed eyes staring at the ceiling. "See? That's dead Aunt Rose," Sam said. "I'm hauling her off to the—"

Anastasia had an idea. "Sam," she whispered, "funerals are supposed to be very private and quiet."

"They are?"

"Yeah. So you have to drive all your cars and trucks real quietly, and you have to whisper."

"Like a secret?" Sam's eyes were wide. He loved secrets.

Anastasia nodded solemnly.

"Oh. Okay," Sam whispered. He turned back to his line of cars and began to move them very quietly. *"Rrrrrr,"* he murmured under his breath.

Relieved, Anastasia headed for the kitchen, where she could hear her parents and Uncle George.

>< >< ><

"Who, what, when, where, and why," Anastasia said as she stirred her corn flakes.

Her father turned another page of the *Boston Globe* and didn't say anything. Her mother took a sip of coffee, added another word to the crossword puzzle she was doing, and didn't say anything.

But Uncle George looked up quizzically from the magazine he was reading. It sure was nice to have company in the house, Anastasia thought; it meant that someone paid *attention* to you now and then.

"I'm practicing to be a journalist," Anastasia explained to Uncle George. "And those are the questions that a good journalist answers right at the beginning of an article."

"Oh, I see," Uncle George said politely, and looked back at his magazine.

"Or a *piece*," Anastasia continued. "A real pro usually calls it a piece instead of an article. For example, right now I'm working on a piece about the seventh-grade girls' basketball team, for our school paper."

"I see," said Uncle George politely, and his eyes sneaked a look back at his magazine article.

"So you see, I have to answer those questions

when I write the piece. I'll show you how it works. Ask me the questions, one by one."

"What? What questions?" Uncle George asked.

"Who, what, when, where, and why," Anastasia explained patiently. "Ask them one at a time."

Uncle George closed his magazine. Good; now he was really paying attention. "Who?" he asked.

"The seventh-grade girls' basketball team," Anastasia replied. "Go on. Ask the next one."

"What?" asked Uncle George.

"Won their fourth game in a row. Go on."

"When?"

"Last Friday afternoon."

"Where?"

"At Lexington Junior High. Okay, next?"

"Why?"

"In continued pursuit of the regional championship. Do you like that phrase, 'continued pursuit'? I thought it up all by myself."

Uncle George nodded. "It's quite, ah, sophisticated. Yes, I like it very much."

Anastasia spooned up the last of her corn flakes and took her empty bowl to the sink. "I'll let you do one more, Uncle George, now that you're getting the hang of it. Start asking the questions again. Start with 'who.'"

Uncle George grinned and said, "Who?"

"Anastasia Krupnik—"

"What?"

"Unfortunately has found it necessary to cancel her plans to visit her friend's new apartment—"

"When?"

"This morning—"

"Where?"

"About half a mile from this house—"

"Why?"

"Because it's raining," Anastasia said angrily. "It's *pouring*, and it's not ever going to stop."

"If your dad will let me borrow his car," Uncle George suggested, "I could give you a ride to your friend's. I don't have any plans this morning."

"*Would* you? Hey, that'd be *great*, Uncle George! Dad, is that okay?"

Myron Krupnik looked up from the newspaper. "Mmmmmm," he muttered, and looked back down.

"I'll just go get my jacket," Anastasia said. "Do you want me to get your jacket out of the guest room, Uncle George? Or maybe a necktie or something?"

Uncle George looked down at the old plaid flannel shirt he was wearing. "Isn't this all right?" he asked. "Do I need a necktie to give you a lift to your friend's?"

"Well, no, I guess not. But I just thought that maybe, on the remote chance that we *might* meet Daphne's very attractive mother—"

Katherine Krupnik looked up from her crossword puzzle. "Anastasia," she said in a warning voice.

"You look just fine, Uncle George," Anastasia said hastily.

Anastasia glanced over at her uncle as he backed the car out of the garage. He really *did* look like Clark Gable, even from the side. He had that nice mustache and a very warm smile.

And widowers, she knew from magazine articles, were by far the best husbands. Much better than divorced men. It was because they remembered their wives fondly, instead of gritting their teeth and writing alimony checks each month. Probably Uncle George remembered Aunt Rose so fondly that already he was wishing he could find somebody just as nice as she had been. Someone like, maybe, Caroline Bellingham, Daphne's mother.

"We go that way, straight ahead, for three blocks, then turn left," Anastasia said as Uncle George pulled out into the street. "I suppose you remember Aunt Rose very fondly," she added.

He shifted gears and the car lurched and sputtered. It was an old, temperamental car. "Straight ahead," he repeated, "and then left after three blocks. Is that what you said?"

"Right. And also I said that I suppose you remember Aunt Rose very fondly."

"Well, ah, yes," Uncle George replied. "Yes, I do. I'm sorry you didn't know her, Anastasia."

"Mom and Dad told me what a nice lady she was. And that you were very happily married."

"Yes, that's true."

"Do you suppose—here, Uncle George; here's where you turn left—do you suppose it will take you a very long time to recover from the shock of her dea— Ah, her passing away?"

Uncle George turned the corner. "It will take time," he said. "It was sudden. Do we go straight now?"

Anastasia nodded. "Straight for half a mile. I'll tell

you when to turn onto Daphne's street. By the way, Daphne's mother is also recovering from the shock of the very sudden loss of her husband."

"Oh? I'm sorry to hear that." Uncle George looked sympathetic in a Clark Gable–ish way. Anastasia hoped he wouldn't ask her the *cause* of the loss of Mrs. Bellingham's husband. The sinister Sal Monella was one thing: grim and tragic. But a fourth-grade Sunday school teacher was something else again.

"Here. Turn right here. This is their street, and their apartment is halfway down the block. It must be that tall building there. Yeah, look, that's Daphne on the front steps, with the umbrella."

Uncle George parked at the curb in front of Daphne's apartment building. He reached over, across Anastasia, and opened the door on her side. Daphne grinned, waved, and came over to the car. She was wearing her huge white shirt, the one that made her look vaguely like the archangel Gabriel, over a pair of jeans, and she was holding an enormous black umbrella.

"This is my Uncle George," Anastasia said proudly. "Uncle George, this is my friend Daphne Bellingham."

"Hi," Daphne said, and she looked at Anastasia. The look meant: You're right. Clark Gable.

"What time would you like me to pick you up, Anastasia?" Uncle George hadn't even stopped the car motor.

"Aren't you coming in? I bet Daphne would love for you to meet her very lovely mother. Especially since you and her mother have so much in common," Anastasia said.

"Yeah, I would," Daphne agreed. "Come in and have a cup of coffee. That's why I brought the umbrella out, to help you get from the car to the front door."

Uncle George made several polite, Clark Gable–like attempts to leave. If this had been *Gone with the Wind,* he would have said, "Frankly, my dear, I don't give a damn." But Anastasia and Daphne continued to hold the car door open, until finally he took the keys out of the ignition. "Just for a minute," he said, and he followed the girls into the building and upstairs to the second floor, where Daphne lived.

Who What When Where Why

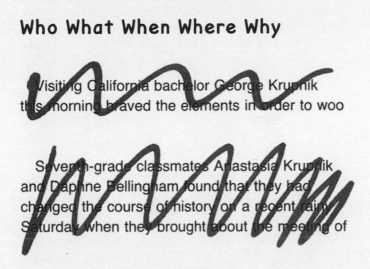

~~Visiting California bachelor George Krupnik this morning braved the elements in order to woo~~

~~Seventh-grade classmates Anastasia Krupnik and Daphne Bellingham found that they had changed the course of history on a recent rainy Saturday when they brought about the meeting of~~

The recent introduction of Los Angeles
bachelor George Krupnik to former Sunday school
teacher Caroline Bellingham did not go,
witnesses report, quite as smoothly as
acquaintances of the couple had hoped.

seven

"*Rats,*" said Anastasia gloomily, "it didn't work. I'm sorry to say this, but your mother really acted like a jerk, Daphne."

"I think she's mentally disturbed," Daphne said matter-of-factly. "She used to act fairly normal. But now she's rude to everybody, the way she was to your Uncle George. Boy, will she be mad when she gets her sanity back and realizes she was rude to someone who looks just like Clark Gable."

They were in Daphne's bedroom in the apartment. It was smaller than her old bedroom had been, with just a tiny closet and one window. And it had hideous wallpaper: pale green, with ladies in hoop skirts, holding parasols beside a lake. But on the whole it wasn't a bad bedroom. Daphne had moved all of her stuff, so that the atmosphere hadn't changed; her posters were there on the walls, and her big stuffed dragon still sat on her bed, the way he had in the old house.

But it was true that Daphne's mother had changed. A *lot*. Back in the old days, when she was the wife of the Congregational minister, she really *acted* like the wife of the Congregational minister. Daphne and Anastasia had both thought she was pretty boring. She sang in the church choir; she served tea to the Altar Guild; she played bridge; she even taught Sunday school for a while. That was weird, Anastasia thought; Mrs. Bellingham had probably attended Sunday school teacher meetings with the very woman who was going to become her husband's girlfriend.

She flopped down on Daphne's bed beside the stuffed dragon and said, "I just had a weird thought. Your mother taught Sunday school right along with the woman who was going to become your father's girlfriend. And she didn't even know it."

Daphne flopped down beside her, on the other side of the dragon. "Yeah, they were friends. So what? Why is that weird?"

"Well," Anastasia said slowly, "it has ramifications."

"Meaning what?"

"Meaning that you and I, at this very moment, could already know the people who are going to play a role in our future. We might know the people we're going to marry, for example."

Daphne made a face. "Speak for yourself. *I'm* not ever going to get married."

"You might change your mind. You used to have a crush on Eddie Fox."

"A crush, sure. Marriage, that's something else again. Look what happened to my parents. Of course, a lot of it was my fault." Daphne stood up and wandered over to the bureau. She picked up a bottle of nail polish. "You want to paint your toenails? I'm going to."

"Okay." Anastasia began unlacing her hiking boots. "What shade is that?"

Daphne read the label. "Fatal Apple."

"That's cool. I used that once before. It has matching lipstick. But I look gross with lipstick on."

They passed the little bottle back and forth and began to paint their toenails. "Don't shake the bed,"

Daphne said. "I always smear nail polish anyway, and it's worse if the bed jiggles."

Silently, meticulously, they did one toenail after another. Anastasia finally stretched out one leg so that she could view her left foot with all five toes done. She grinned. It looked glamorous. It looked like someone else's foot. It looked like the foot of a model in the bathing suit issue of *Sports Illustrated*. It looked like a foot that could climb a rope. It looked like—

"Hey," she said suddenly, turning to Daphne. "What did you mean, it was your fault? I just remembered that you said that. Your parents' divorce was your fault?"

Daphne blew on her toes to dry the polish. "Yeah, they say it wasn't, but I know otherwise."

"How could it be your fault?"

"Remember when you first met me, right after you moved to town? Remember how weird I was?"

Anastasia thought back. She remembered. She remembered the time Daphne had given the cat a mohawk, and the way she had painted her bedroom walls black. She remembered all the times Daphne had been in detention at school.

"I wouldn't call it weird, Daph. You were being adolescent."

Daphne sighed. She bent her knees, rested her arms on them, and put her head down in her arms. "I know," she muttered. "But I wish I hadn't been. They couldn't deal with it. And now look."

"Look at what? Come on, Daphne. Your parents dealt with it very well. They never got upset or anything. *My* parents would have gone berserk-o if I had painted my walls black. Yours just waited till you got tired of such a sick-looking room and then they took the price of yellow paint out of your allowance. In my opinion that was an absolutely intelligent thing to do, much better than yelling, which is what my parents would have done."

"You think?" Daphne turned her head and looked up at Anastasia.

"I *know*."

"I always thought your parents were terrific. I thought it was neat that they yelled at you and stuff. My parents never, *ever* yelled at me. And guess what—" Daphne put her head back down in her arms. She started to cry. "I wanted them to."

Anastasia sat silently and watched Daphne's shoulders move as she cried. She wondered what to do. People on TV always knew what to do, what to say. Joanne Woodward always knew just how to say soothing, intelligent things when she was playing psychiatrist roles. And Anastasia never did.

"You're shaking the bed," she said finally. "You told me not to shake the bed, and now *you're* shaking the bed."

Daphne took a deep breath and tried to stop crying.

"Here," said Anastasia, and she handed Daphne a tissue from the box of Kleenex on a nearby table. "Psychiatrists on TV are always giving people Kleenex when they cry. Maybe I should become a psychiatrist."

Daphne blew her nose. She took another deep breath. "I'm sorry," she said. "I'm a jerk."

"No, you're not. I don't mind that you cried. You don't have to be embarrassed or anything," Anastasia told her. "I just feel bad that I can't think of anything to say or to do. Except to tell you that I'm positive it wasn't your fault that your parents got divorced.

"I'll do a journalistic evaluation," Anastasia suggested. "I'm going to ask you these questions: who, what, when, where, and why. First one is 'who,' and you say your parents' names. Ready? Who?"

Daphne smiled a little. "Reverend and Mrs. John Bellingham," she said.

"What?" Anastasia asked next.

"Filed for divorce—"

"When?"

"Last month—"

"Where?"

Daphne wasn't sure. "Boston, I suppose. Some courtroom."

"Why? Be honest, now."

Daphne took one more deep breath. "Well, because as time went along and they got older, their personalities didn't seem to match very well anymore. Like, my mom didn't want to teach Sunday school or sing in the choir anymore, or go to all those meetings. But my dad really thought she ought to. He said it was her duty. But she wanted to get a job, because she had all this education and everything—she had applied to law school way back, before they got married, but then she never went—and my dad said it wasn't appropriate for the rector's wife to work, and they didn't need the money—" She stopped for a moment, took another breath, and went on. "And he didn't understand that it wasn't the *money;* it was, well, my mom said it was the self-esteem. But he said it ought to be enough self-esteem to be the wife of the minister of the largest Congregational church in the whole county, and when he said that, my mom swore at him—I'm not going to say what she said—"

Anastasia giggled. "Why not? I've heard you swear lots of times."

"Yeah, but nobody ever heard my *mom* swear, and I'm not going to ruin her image. Anyway, then she said they ought to see a marriage counselor, and he said, 'By God, I *am* a marriage counselor! And you should respect that!' and that's when she called him a sanctimonious creep, and he said—"

"Hey, wait, Daph—how do you know all this? They didn't say it in front of *you,* did they?"

Daphne shook her head. "I eavesdropped," she said. "From my bedroom closet, if I pushed the win-

- 81 -

ter stuff aside and got up close to the wall, I could hear everything they were saying in their bedroom. It was a rotten thing to do, I suppose."

"But necessary," Anastasia said. "I can understand that."

Daphne wiped her eyes with the back of her hand. "Anyway, that's about all of the 'why,' I guess."

Anastasia looked at her in astonishment. "Well, that proves it! Don't you see, Daphne?"

"See what?"

"All those conversations you eavesdropped on — and they never knew you were listening, did they?"

"No. I always shoved the clothes back where they belonged, so my mother wouldn't notice."

"Well, they never mentioned you. Did they *once* say, 'And that rotten kid Daphne — which one of us gets stuck with *her?*'"

Daphne giggled. "No," she said. "They mentioned me, of course. But it was always just how concerned they were about me."

Anastasia stood up and looked down at her bare Fatal Apple toes. "Well," she said, "quit being a jerk. It wasn't your fault. How do your toes look?"

Daphne stood up and looked down at her own

feet. "Sexy," she decided. "Maybe I will get married someday, after all."

Uncle George beeped the horn of the car after he pulled up to the curb. He didn't even come up and ring the doorbell of the apartment. And no wonder. When he came up before, Mrs. Bellingham had said, "How do you do, you'll have to excuse me, I'm busy," very coolly. Then she went to her bedroom, and Uncle George sat there on the living room couch, drinking a cup of coffee very awkwardly while Anastasia and Daphne tried to make conversation.

"Hi, Uncle George," Anastasia said after she dashed through the rain and got into the car. "Thanks for coming to pick me up."

"Forgive me for not ringing the bell," he said, "but I think that woman didn't like me."

Anastasia rolled her eyes. "She was just acting weird, Uncle George. She just lost her husband and everything, and she's acting a little weird. I think she'll get over it."

"Your friend Daphne is charming," Uncle George added. "And she has the most beautiful hair. It reminds me of Shirley Temple."

Oh, gross. Anastasia could never tell Daphne that. Elderly people like Uncle George—and even Anastasia's parents—all liked those old Shirley Temple movies, where she danced around, smiling, showing her dimples—and sometimes her underpants, talk about *gross*—with her curls bouncing.

Daphne, in fact—since she did happen to have the same sort of curls—had once, for a school talent assembly, mouthed the words of "On the Good Ship Lollipop" to a record, while she danced, wearing a short ruffled dress. But one of her front teeth was blacked out, and she was wearing a black lace garter belt, which showed every time she did a little Shirley Temple twirl.

The entire junior high had thought it was hysterical, and Daphne had gotten a standing ovation. But everybody over the age of thirty-five—which included a lot of the teachers—thought it was sacrilegious or something. Daphne almost ended up in detention again.

Ms. Wilhelmina Willoughby, Anastasia remembered with satisfaction, had loved it.

Thinking of Ms. Wilhelmina Willoughby reminded Anastasia that she planned to spend the remainder of the Saturday afternoon out in the garage once again. She had decided to try wearing her mother's gardening gloves this time, since her hands were beginning to be sore from all the rope-climbing attempts.

Who What When Where Why

On a rainy Saturday morning, young Anastasia Krupnik showed remarkable psychiatric skill, almost as wisdom-filled and sensitive as Joanne Woodward, when she

Although the greatly anticipated uncle-mother meeting did not go exactly as well as they had hoped, Anastasia Krupnik and Daphne Bellingham spent a pleasant morning recently

Daphne Bellingham was revealed recently as a complete idiot as far as her insight into her parents' divorce was concerned, noted psychotherapist Anastasia Krupnik said Saturday. "I straightened her out," Krupnik, who is noted for her tact and sensitivity, said to reporters.

eight

PHWEET! Ms. Willoughby's whistle blasted through the gym on Monday afternoon, and the basketball game stopped. Everywhere there was the rubbery sound of sneakers coming to a speedy halt against the floor. Meredith Halberg bounced the basketball once and tossed it ineffectually toward the basket, and it rolled over into the corner where the gymnastics mats were piled.

"The period's almost over," Ms. Willoughby called. "But gather 'round for a minute before you go to the locker room."

The seventh-grade girls, still panting from the basketball game, clustered around Ms. Willoughby.

Anastasia stood a little to the side. Somehow, in gym, she felt a little separate from her classmates. She watched them now, each in a bright blue gym suit, listening to the gym teacher.

"Very shortly," Ms. Willoughby was saying, "the day after tomorrow, to be exact, there will be a team of educators from several other countries visiting our school. You probably know that already."

Everybody burst out laughing. The entire school had been talking of nothing else for two weeks. There were posters everywhere, reminding the students about the coming visit by the team of educators. The principal had spoken about it in a special assembly. Every single teacher had devoted a long discussion to it.

All the teachers and administrators, Anastasia realized, were *terrified* that somehow or other they were going to be disgraced and humiliated in front of the foreign educators. Eddie Fox might yell out something obscene, the way he did occasionally. Daphne Bellingham — although it had been months since she had done it in assembly — might suddenly be moved to do her Shirley Temple imitation again, in the middle of a history class. Eighth graders would all light up cigarettes in the halls instead of sneaking them in the bathroom the way they usually did.

All of it was highly unlikely. The junior high students were actually a nice bunch of kids, and they wanted to impress the foreign visitors favorably. But Anastasia could see that the entire faculty was very nervous. And now Ms. Willoughby (Anastasia had supposed that such a super-cool person was above that sort of nervousness, but apparently not) was going to give the "Let's be very impressive for our visitors" pep talk, too.

"We'll be doing a demonstration for them," Ms. Willoughby was saying. "We won't have a lot of time because they'll just be coming in small groups through the gym briefly. But physical education is very important in Europe—you remember how the Germans and Rumanians always perform at the summer Olympics?—so they'll be particularly interested in what goes on in gym.

"I want you all to take your gym suits home for laundering tonight. And *iron* them!"

Everyone groaned.

"White socks," Ms. Willoughby went on. "No argyle knee socks, Jennifer Billings!"

Everyone laughed at Jenny Billings's bright yellow, green, and red knee socks.

"No pantyhose, Daphne Bellingham," Ms. Willoughby announced, and Daphne said, "Okay, okay."

"*White socks*. No jewelry—that means you too, Jill, even though you like to jangle—all three sets of earrings have to go. Be on time Wednesday, everyone. Let's see, what else?" Ms. Willoughby looked down at her clipboard.

Jenny Billings raised her hand. "You said we'll be doing a demonstration. What are we going to demonstrate?"

"Oh," Ms. Willoughby said, "you're what, second period?" She moved her finger down the paper on the clipboard. "First period, folk dancing; third period, precision marching. You guys are going to do rope-climbing. Now—we're running late. Class dismissed!" *Phweet!* Her whistle blew again.

"Anastasia," Ms. Willoughby called as the girls all ran toward the locker room door, "could I see you for a minute?"

"The whistle!" Anastasia said, choking back sobs. "She said I could be in charge of blowing the whistle! Just as if I were a little kid, you know, like Sam, who could be conned into thinking that blowing the whistle was a real important job. And she was so nice about it, I couldn't argue or anything, and I know she—"

"Shhh," her mother said soothingly. "Don't cry." She stroked Anastasia's hair. "Let me think. I'm sure we can work something out."

"I could just be absent," Anastasia suggested, sniffling. "But I *want* to be there when those people from other countries come. I really want them to see what a neat school we have, and in English class I'm supposed to recite a poem when they're there, so I *can't* be absent. No one else knows that poem but me—"

Sam looked up from the floor, where he was playing. "I can do a poem," he announced. "Listen: 'I'm Popeye the sailor man, I live in a garbage can—'"

"MOM! Make him *stop!*" Anastasia wailed.

"Sam," Mrs. Krupnik said firmly, "shhhh. Anastasia's upset. You just play with your cars and be quiet. Have a nice, quiet funeral. You can bury Aunt Rose over there, under that stack of canvases."

Sam nodded, eyed the stack of canvases against the far wall of his mother's studio, and loaded the blank-eyed G.I. Joe onto the back of his dump truck. *"Rrrrr,"* he said, and began driving away slowly.

Mrs. Krupnik turned back to Anastasia. "I wonder if he'll get tired of funerals by the time George goes back to California," she murmured. "Four more days."

"*Two* more days till the rope-climbing demonstration," Anastasia said bitterly. "I suppose I should practice up on whistle-blowing."

"No, wait," her mother said. She put down the pen she'd been holding and looked at the drawing on the table in front of her. "This job isn't due at the publisher until the tenth of the month. That gives me a couple of weeks still, so I can set it aside for a little while without feeling too guilty. What time is it?"

"Four o'clock," Anastasia said, looking at her watch.

"Sam's busy with his macabre game, aren't you, Sam? Are you keeping busy over there?"

Sam looked up from the canvases, where he had just disposed of Aunt Rose. "'I always go swimmin' with bare-naked women,'" he said. "That's the rest of my poem about Popeye."

"Sam is busy. George is reading in the study, Dad's

not home yet from work, and dinner preparations can wait for a little while. So, Anastasia, out we go to the garage," her mother concluded. "It's you and me, kid; we're going to beat that rope if it kills us."

"Really?" Anastasia stood up and brushed her hair out of her eyes.

"*Really,*" her mother responded. "Ask me 'Who?'"

"Who?"

"Anastasia Krupnik—" said her mother.

"What?"

"Mastered the difficult art of rope-climbing—"

"When?" Anastasia was grinning.

"This very afternoon—"

"Where?"

"In the Krupnik garage—"

"Why?"

"Because she wasn't about to be the only kid in the seventh grade who was assigned to whistle-blowing, not in front of Ms. Wilhelmina Willoughby, the most glamorous gym teacher in town, and a whole band of visiting foreigners. And because her mother was *determined* that she would do it!"

>< >< ><

"My arms ache," Anastasia told her mother that night.

"Of course they do," her mother replied. "You really gave them a workout."

They were sitting together in the study, after Sam had gone to bed. From the kitchen they could hear the sound of dishes rattling and the laughter of Dr. Krupnik and his brother. It was Anastasia's father's night to do the dishes, and Uncle George was helping, even though Uncle George said that in thirty years of marriage, Aunt Rose had never once asked him to wash a single dish.

"Not even *one?* Not even maybe an ashtray or something?" Anastasia had asked in disbelief.

"Nope, not one." Uncle George shook his head.

"Good grief. Dad has to do them two nights a week. It's part of our family rules. Of course," Anastasia added, "every family is different." But she had added that only to be polite. Secretly, she thought that any family in which the husband never washed a single dish in thirty years was *extremely* weird, even if he *did* look like Clark Gable.

Anastasia wondered if the real Clark Gable had ever washed the dishes—before he died, of course. Did he come home from the movie studio, take off his Rhett Butler costume and makeup, eat supper with his wife, and then wash the dishes? Probably not. Probably his wife didn't either. They would have had a maid, Anastasia decided. Or else they ate takeout food: Kentucky Fried Chicken, or pizza, or Chinese food, every night. Anastasia sometimes wished that her family were rich enough to eat takeout food every single night.

Maybe up in heaven, the real Clark Gable would run into Aunt Rose. She would notice how much he looked like Uncle George, of course, and she would introduce herself, and they could have dinner together or something.

No, they'd go to a movie, Anastasia decided. Not dinner. Aunt Rose probably wasn't into going out to dinner, not after her recent experience with Sal Monella.

"You look so much like my husband," Aunt Rose would say to Clark Gable.

No, that wasn't right. My *late* husband? But "late" meant that the person had died. And Uncle George hadn't died—Aunt Rose had.

"You look so much like my early husband," she might say. Maybe that was the way it worked.

"Anastasia?"

It was her mother's voice. Anastasia shook herself awake and was surprised to find that she was still sitting on the couch in the study.

"Sweetie, you fell asleep. Maybe you ought to go on up to bed. You really wore yourself out this afternoon in the garage."

Anastasia stood up groggily. "Yeah, I think I'll go to bed.

"Mom?" she asked, as she turned to go upstairs. "I'm really doing a lot better, aren't I? On the rope, I mean. I got about halfway up that last time. Maybe even three-quarters of the way up. Didn't I?"

Her mother nodded. "I'm sure you got halfway, Anastasia. And tomorrow, when you practice again, you'll go even farther."

Who What When Where Why

Unaware that her prize student had secretly been practicing, noted gym teacher Wilhelmina Willoughby neglected to

In preparation for the upcoming visit of foreign educators, Anastasia Krupnik, 13, was assigned the important task of

Ordinarily a perceptive and sensitive person, Ms. Wilhelmina Willoughby had somehow overlooked the increasing skill which seventh-grader Anastasia Krupnik was developing at the difficult feat of rope-climbing, which she probably would master by Wednesday's demonstration, which did not really require a student whistle-blower.

nine

"O world,'" recited Anastasia dramatically, "'I cannot hold thee close enough!'"

"Hold it," Mr. Rafferty said. "I wonder if a gesture would be appropriate there. If you sort of *flung* your arms out . . ."

Anastasia cringed. "I don't think I'm the flinging sort, Mr. Rafferty," she said.

"Well," he replied with a disappointed sigh, "all right. Go on."

"'Thy winds! Thy wide gray skies!'" Anastasia went on.

"Maybe if you flung your arms out there, on 'skies' . . ."

Anastasia groaned inwardly. Mr. Rafferty really was into emoting. She didn't mind *saying* the poem in front of the visiting educators—she didn't even have stage fright anymore, practicing in front of the class. But she sure wasn't going to emote, and fling her arms around.

It was, Anastasia thought, really a neat poem. Imagine actually writing that: "O world, I cannot hold thee close enough!" Anastasia had *felt* like that a lot—happy, and in love with the whole world—but she never in a million years would have thought of the right words, the way the poet had.

On the other hand, Anastasia's father—himself a pretty famous poet—had not reacted very well to her recitation when she had practiced at home. He had made a terrible face.

"It's not *you*, sport," he said. "You're doing just fine. It's the poem. That poem is sentimental garbage. Why don't they assign you something great to memorize?"

"Like what? It has to be something uplifting."

He stared at her with a puzzled look. "Why uplifting?"

Anastasia shrugged. "I don't know. Because these people from other countries are visiting, and we're supposed to be real patriotic and happy and enthusiastic and uplifting."

"Like Nazi Youth?"

"*Dad!* Cut it out!"

Dr. Krupnik began to fill his pipe. "Sorry," he said. "I don't know why I said an obnoxious thing like that. Isn't it amazing how sometimes obnoxious remarks just *appear* out of your mouth without any warning? I'd better keep my mouth shut. But I *do* think it's one of the worst poems ever written. That's a matter of taste, of course."

Anastasia giggled. "Yeah. Like Sam's favorite poem is 'Popeye the Sailor Man.'"

Standing now in front of her English class, Anastasia wondered briefly what would happen if someone decided to recite "Popeye the Sailor Man" in front of the visiting educators. Well, it wouldn't be Anastasia Krupnik. She *liked* "O World—" and she would do her best with it tomorrow, even though she would cool it on the gestures.

"All right, Anastasia," Mr. Rafferty said. "That's just fine. I wish you'd *think* about the arm-flinging, though. Maybe you'll change your mind. Or maybe, when you're actually reciting the poem for an audience, the emotions will overwhelm you and the gestures will come naturally."

She nodded politely and went back to her desk. No way was arm-flinging ever going to come naturally, not to Anastasia Krupnik.

Gym class was a severe humiliation. The only good thing about gym class was that the students got to wear jeans for a change, since their gym suits were all at home being laundered for the next day's demonstration.

But Ms. Willoughby didn't even let Anastasia *try* the ropes. She handed Anastasia the whistle, and put her in charge while her classmates climbed the ropes.

"Ms. Willoughby," Anastasia began, "I practiced last night in my garage, and I think maybe I can—"

But Ms. Willoughby—beautiful, sensitive, kind, thoughtful Ms. Wilhelmina Willoughby—was already headed off for the other side of the gym to pick up some basketballs. She was determined that the gym look perfect for tomorrow.

Grouchily Anastasia turned toward the lines of

waiting girls. She put the whistle's cord around her neck, lifted the whistle to her mouth, and blew. *Phweet!* Then she watched, dejected, while her classmates and friends all clambered up the ropes like chimpanzees.

She *had* begun to master the rope in the garage, Anastasia thought on her way home from school. Yesterday, with her mother cheering her on, she had gotten halfway up. If only Ms. Willoughby had stopped worrying about the appearance of the gym long enough to listen.

Anastasia shifted her schoolbooks from one arm to the other and began to daydream. There, in front of a whole group — maybe a hundred or more — of visiting international educators (all wearing uniforms, for some reason, in Anastasia's fantasy, and taking notes in small notebooks), Anastasia would step forward, still holding the hated whistle, after the rope-climbing exhibition was over.

"Now," she would say (and they would all look up, startled, from their notes), "one final demonstration!"

Phweet! Phweet! She would blow the whistle briskly, twice. In the corner, she could see Ms. Wilhelmina Willoughby watching with amazement and awe.

"I owe this all to Ms. Wilhelmina Willoughby," Anastasia would announce. Then she would remove the whistle and its cord from around her neck. "Everything that I am, I owe to Ms. Willoughby." Perhaps there would be a smattering of applause then, and Ms. Willoughby would blush and acknowledge it gracefully with a nod.

Anastasia would step forward to the rope. With one quick leap she would grasp it with both hands, and her sneakered feet would instantly find their grip. Up she would go: so smoothly, so lithely, so quickly that the audience would hold its collective breath. From high above them, she would hear the *"Ooooooh"* as she nimbly performed her most amazing feat, something never attempted before in the junior high gym. She would move from one rope to the next, and then the next: back and forth between the six ropes, like an acrobat, her toes pointed, twirling now and then, extending one arm gracefully, looking down with a poised smile.

A sequinned outfit with pink tights would be better, Anastasia realized, than a royal blue gym suit. But no matter. The costume wasn't the important thing. The important thing was the skill, the daring, the absolute fearlessness and agility with which she dazzled the crowd below.

"I dedicate this next stunt—" she would call. No, wait; "stunt" wasn't right. "I dedicate this next *feat* to that most illustrious gym teacher, Ms. Wilhelmina Willoughby!"

Silence would fall upon the awed crowd. Anastasia would look down to see Ms. Willoughby's face, rapt with pleasure, pride, and delight, looking up at her.

Let's see. What would the feat be? Maybe she could leap, no hands, from one rope—somersaulting in the air—over to the top of the basketball backboard, soaring through the—

CRASH. Anastasia's daydream ended abruptly because she had stumbled on the back steps of her own house. Two months of math homework papers had flown out of her notebook into the rhododendron bushes. She had ripped one knee of her jeans, and her elbow felt scraped. The best sticker on the cover of her notebook was torn.

Hastily, from the spot where she was sprawled on the steps, Anastasia glanced around. Next door,

Mrs. Stein's curtains were drawn. Good. She hadn't seen it. No one was passing in the street or on the front sidewalk. The Krupniks' kitchen windows were empty; the garage doors were closed; Sam's tricycle was parked in a corner of the driveway, but he was nowhere in sight.

What a relief. No one had noticed what a colossal fool she had made of herself. Anastasia began to pick up the scattered books and papers quickly, before anyone could come along and ask what had happened. Just as she had thrust the last of the math papers back into her notebook, the kitchen door opened and Uncle George looked out.

"Oh, hi, Anastasia," he said. "Is everything okay? I was listening to your dad's Billie Holiday records and suddenly I heard a thump."

Anastasia stood up and smiled, even though her elbow and knee both throbbed. "Everything's fine, Uncle George," she said. "I was just practicing a little precision marching routine that we do in gym class." *Thump, thump;* Anastasia held her head up high and marched firmly up the back steps and through the door, which her uncle was holding open.

"That's pretty good," Uncle George said in an admiring voice. "It reminds me of when I was in the Marines thirty-five years ago."

"Yes, well, I owe it all to my gym teacher," Anastasia replied. She continued marching right through the kitchen and into the bathroom to apply some wet Kleenex to her bleeding elbow.

That night, despite her still-aching wounds, alone in the garage, Anastasia did it. She got to the halfway point, the way she had the previous afternoon, and she just kept going. Somehow it was suddenly easy; her feet grabbed the rope just right, and her hands moved one after the other the way they were supposed to, and she didn't panic and didn't slow down—and it worked. She went all the way to the top, touched the beam up there by the ceiling, and lowered herself back down.

"I did it!" she shrieked, dashing into the kitchen where her parents and uncle were lingering over their after-dinner coffee. "Look!"

She held up her index finger, covered with dust from the top of the old beam. "I got all the way to the top!"

Her mother hugged her. "Congratulations!" she said. "I knew you could!"

"A-plus," her father said proudly. "I knew you could too."

Uncle George shook her hand.

"I have to call Daphne," Anastasia said. "Excuse me." She went to the telephone in the study.

"*Great,*" Daphne said when she heard the news. "I really felt sorry for you in gym, Anastasia. It's really crummy when everybody else can do something and you can't. I felt that way once at summer camp before I learned to swim. I was still in Advanced Beginners and every single other person my age was in Junior Lifesaving."

"Do you think I ought to call Ms. Willoughby and tell her, so that I won't have to do the whistle tomorrow when all those visitors are there?"

"Call a teacher at home? That's kind of a weird thought. I suppose you could, if she's in the phone book, but— Hey, Anastasia, I have a better idea!"

"What?"

"Surprise her, and everybody. Just wait till everyone else has done it, and then—heck, you've got the whistle—just announce one final event, and it'll be *you!* That'll blow Willoughby's mind; she thinks you're so uncoordinated."

It was just like Anastasia's latest daydream. Imagine that, thought Anastasia: a daydream that can turn into reality. Boy, there aren't very many of those!

"Do you think she'd get mad?"

"Willoughby? Mad?" Daphne hooted. "She never gets mad, Anastasia. She'd *love* it."

Anastasia decided that Daphne was probably right. Maybe she would do it. *Probably* she would do it. Just like the daydream.

Who What When Where Why

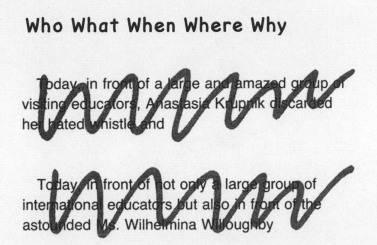

Today, in front of a large and amazed group of
visiting educators, Anastasia Krupnik discarded
her hated whistle and

Today, in front of not only a large group of
international educators but also in front of the
astounded Ms. Wilhelmina Willoughby

Despite injuries sustained during practice,
today a new gymnastic star was born when
Anastasia Krupnik, 13, astounded a large
audience, which included Ms. Wilhelmina Willoughby,
by discarding her whistle and taking to the ropes
as if she had been born to chimpanzees.

ten

For once, Anastasia didn't wear jeans to school. The students hadn't been told to wear anything special on Wednesday, but most of them did anyway. The boys seemed to be wearing chinos instead of jeans, and sport shirts with creases ironed into the sleeves. Many of the girls were wearing dresses or skirts.

Lesley Ann Roth, who always, always, *always* wore the same Jordache jeans and a Brown University sweatshirt to school, was wearing a Laura Ashley dress. Anastasia looked with surprise at Lesley Ann's legs, and whispered to Daphne, "She actually has skin! I thought she was completely made out of denim!"

Daphne whispered back, "That dress cost ninety-something dollars. I tried it on once at the store, but my mother wouldn't buy it for me. She said that ninety Ethiopians could eat for a month on that."

Anastasia giggled. She pictured Ethiopians munching on the flower-sprigged Laura Ashley dress, even though she knew that wasn't what Mrs. Bellingham had meant.

Anastasia didn't really like dresses herself. They made her feel self-conscious. But this year, in seventh grade, she had been observing Ms. Willoughby's layered look very closely; and at home, secretly in her room, she tried to imitate it. So far it hadn't ever worked. When she put on a leotard, and over it a denim skirt, and over that a paisley wraparound skirt (sneaked out of her mother's closet), and on top a turtleneck shirt, with a cotton blouse over that, and a suede vest (sneaked out of her father's closet) on top of that — well, she groaned when she looked into the full-length mirror on the back of her door. She looked like a bag lady. She looked like a sausage. She looked like a person wearing six layers of clothing — which was exactly what she was. But why did Ms. Willoughby look so glamorous when *she* wore six layers of clothing?

It was simply one of those life mysteries that Anastasia had begun to think might never be solved. Today she had given up her experiments and was wearing only her boring denim skirt with a boring striped blouse.

But she felt terrific. She felt terrific because she was somebody who was going to recite a terrific poem in front of a group of very important visiting European educators, and after that she was somebody who was *maybe*—if she decided to do it—going to surprise an entire gym full of people, including Ms. Wilhelmina Willoughby, by climbing a rope. "'O world,'" Anastasia murmured to herself, smiling, "'I cannot hold thee close enough!'"

There was no sign of the visitors in the school, no hint of their presence in homeroom while attendance was being taken. Maybe they didn't come, Anastasia thought anxiously. Maybe their plane was late.

But then the intercom crackled and the principal's voice began an announcement. "Good morning, students," she said much more politely than usual. "I know you all want to join me in welcoming today's visitors, the International Commission for Educational Excellence. Just think: Two days ago they were in Brussels, Belgium, visiting a school, and tomorrow they will be in Indianapolis! Aren't we *fortunate* that they've chosen *our* school as their only stop in the New England area!"

Quit gushing, Mrs. Atkins, Anastasia thought. Go back to being your own normal sarcastic self. How about your usual big lectures about litter in the halls or graffiti in the bathrooms? How about announcing the lunch menu — canned wax beans and cold pizza slices — so that the International Commission for Educational Excellence might consider sending nutritional aid?

But Mrs. Atkins had disappeared from the intercom, and it was time for Anastasia to gather her books and go to English class.

Even Mr. Rafferty had dressed for the occasion, and instead of his usual rumpled, ink-stained clothing, he was wearing a neatly pressed dark suit and a necktie with tiny sailboats on it. "Good morning, class," he said nervously as the seventh graders filed in.

In the back of the room, against a little-used blackboard, six strangers, four men and two women, were standing. They were holding notebooks, exactly as they had in one of Anastasia's fantasies. But they weren't wearing uniforms. They were wearing ordinary clothes. They looked like ordinary people. Anastasia smiled shyly at one of the women, who seemed to be looking at her, and the woman smiled back.

"Today, class," Mr. Rafferty announced, "instead of our usual work on grammar and punctuation, I believe we will try some poetry recitation."

Several students snickered. Mr. Rafferty was trying to make it sound as if he had just casually decided on poetry. Actually, he'd been browbeating them for three weeks to get those assigned poems memorized.

"O world—" thought Anastasia. She knew the poem absolutely by heart. She could almost say it backwards. She hoped that Mr. Rafferty would call on her first.

But he didn't. "Emily Ewing?" he said.

Teacher's pet, straight-A, flawless-skinned, gets-to-go-to-Bermuda-every-Easter Emily Ewing went to the front of the room. Her long, straight dark hair was absolutely smooth and shiny. Once Anastasia had read an ad in a magazine, an ad for some strange religion run by a guy in California. It promised "Perfect

- 114 -

Happiness." Anastasia remembered thinking, when she read it, that she didn't need to go to California and join that religion; she would have Perfect Happiness if only she could make her hair look like Emily Ewing's.

Emily Ewing smiled politely at the visiting educators grouped in the back of the room and began to recite her poem.

Whose woods these are I think I know.
His house is in the village though . . .

Anastasia yawned surreptitiously, cupping her hand over her mouth, while Emily went on and on through the verses of the poem. It was, actually, a pretty good poem. Anastasia wouldn't have minded if Mr. Rafferty had assigned it to her instead of "O World."

Emily did what Mr. Rafferty had suggested, speaking almost in a whisper since the poem was about snowy, quiet woods.

"'And miles to go before I sleep,'" she whispered at the conclusion. "'And miles to go before I sleep.'" Then she smiled again at the back of the room — good grief, Anastasia thought; she almost *curtseyed* — and went back to her desk.

Now maybe he'll call on me. Krupnik, Krupnik,

Krupnik, Anastasia thought, attempting to use ESP on Mr. Rafferty.

But Mr. Rafferty didn't get a chance. One of the visiting educators—one of the men—spoke, in what sounded like a German accent. His *w*'s all came out like *v*'s.

"Ve vould like to qvestion Miss—vat vas it, Youving?"

Mr. Rafferty looked startled. Emily Ewing looked even *more* startled. She turned, in her desk, toward the back of the room.

"Vould you stand, please?" the man asked.

Emily Ewing stood.

"Tell us, please, vhy you tink dis poet repeated dat last line. Am I correct, no odder lines are repeated in dis poem?"

"Yessir, that's right," Emily said.

The man waited for her to respond to his question. Emily looked panic-stricken. The six educators all had their little notebooks and their pens poised.

Mr. Rafferty looked suddenly pale. His mouth formed a wan and sickly smile. "Emily?" he said.

"Well, ah, I guess Frost repeated that last line because all the other stanzas had four lines each, and if he hadn't said that line twice, then there would only have been three lines in that last . . ." Her voice trailed off uncertainly.

"But don't you see," the man went on, "dat makes for a different rhyme pattern in dat final stanza? Vhy vould he do dat? Maybe"—the man gave an odd little chuckle—"he vas a stupid poet?"

"Oh, no, I don't think so," Emily said miserably. "But I don't know why he did that with the last stanza."

"Tank you," the man said. He looked at his colleagues. They all nodded. They all made notes in their notebooks. Emily sat down.

Call on me, call on me, call on me, Anastasia ESPed to Mr. Rafferty. She could see that he was looking around the room, trying to decided whom to call on next. I know my whole poem perfectly, she tried to signal to him telepathically, and I can answer any question they ask me. I *know* I can.

But Mr. Rafferty called on Jacob Berman, the biggest wimp in the class.

Jacob shuffled to the front of the room, stood there with his miserable posture, adjusted his glasses, took a deep breath, and said in his singsong voice:

The sea is calm tonight.
The tide is full, the moon lies fair . . .

The visiting educators all smiled with satisfaction and nodded, recognizing the poem. Anastasia groaned inwardly, recognizing it also, because it was the longest one that anyone had been assigned. Jacob Berman was noted throughout the seventh grade for two things: his disgusting habit of picking his nose and his phenomenal memory. Anastasia was quite certain that Mr. Rafferty had called on Jacob simply because he *knew* that Jacob wouldn't forget a line of that endless poem.

Rats. Jacob droned on and on and Anastasia glanced at the clock. They'd never have time to get through the entire class. She hoped she would be next.

"'Ah, love, let us be true to one another!'" Jacob intoned. The class snickered. Jacob Berman saying "Ah, love, let us be true to one another!" was the most ridiculous thing *ever,* and if all those European guests hadn't been in the back of the room, the students would have fallen out of their desks, laughing.

Finally he was finished. Now me, thought Anastasia. Now me.

But one of the women, a gray-haired lady in a flowered silk dress, said, "Mr. Berman, is it?"

Jacob nodded awkwardly.

"An admirable presentation. But let us look now at the reference to Sophocles in stanza two," the woman said in a clipped, no-nonsense British accent. "Let's consider why Matthew Arnold might have used that reference."

Anastasia could see Mr. Rafferty tense up and then relax as Jacob started in on one of the thoroughly boring explanations that he drew from his incredible memory.

"Well, Sophocles was a Greek dramatist, of course; I think there are seven great tragedies attributed to him in the fourth century B.C.," Jacob began. "So he was no stranger to human misery—which of course Arnold refers to a few lines further along." Anastasia could see the educators scribbling furiously in their little notebooks.

The heck with human misery, Anastasia thought. How about human *joy?* How about "O world! I cannot hold thee close enough"?

"—and if you compare Sophocles' *Antigone*," Jacob was saying, "you'll find a surprising similarity of language, especially in line six of the Arnold poem . . ."

Mr. Rafferty was beaming and beaming and beaming. The educators were all hunched over their little notebooks. Emily Ewing was sulking at her desk. The other students all looked bored.

And then—Anastasia could hardly believe it, but she looked at the clock, and sure enough, it was time—the bell rang and the period was over.

Who What When Where Why

Visiting educators at the local junior high school this morning missed a rare treat, when time failed to permit

An inordinate amount of time taken up by Jacob Berman and his interminable discussion of a Matthew Arnold poem was this morning the cause of

Anastasia Krupnik, 13, disappointed by time limitations which prevented her recitation of a poem in English class, this morning conceived a scheme which would astound not only the visiting international educators but also her own classmates, even Daphne Bellingham, and also her gym teacher, Ms. Wilhelmina Willoughby.

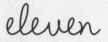

eleven

oy, was I glad Rafferty didn't call on me," Sonya Isaacson giggled as they left the English class. "I
know I would have goofed my poem up."

"I didn't even know mine," Daphne confessed. "I
was going to memorize it last night, but I watched a
movie on HBO instead."

"Anyway, of *course* he'd call on Emily and Jacob,
those nerds," Meredith said. "Look at my gross gym
suit. My mother ironed all these creases into it." She
held up the folded blue gym suit and made a face.

"Willoughby'll love it," Daphne said. "Hey, Anastasia, have you decided what you're going to do for
the gym demonstration?"

"What do you mean?" Sonya asked. "Anastasia

has to blow the whistle while we all make fools of ourselves climbing ropes."

Daphne grinned. "Anastasia has a surprise," she said.

"What? What is it?" Sonya and Meredith turned to Anastasia. "What's the surprise?"

But Anastasia shook her head. She didn't want to talk about it. She was depressed about English class. She had rehearsed and rehearsed and rehearsed that poem. She had overcome her normal self-consciousness to the point that she had desperately *wanted* to recite that poem, that day, to that class, in front of that group of visitors.

The warning bell rang. "You go ahead," Anastasia said to her friends. "I'll catch up."

"Don't be late," Meredith said. "We all promised Ms. Willoughby we'd be on time."

Anastasia nodded glumly. She wanted to walk to gym by herself. She wanted to think.

Probably, she knew, she shouldn't disrupt the gym class in front of all the visitors, maybe embarrassing Ms. Willoughby. She should just be a good sport and blow the whistle the way she'd been told.

If she'd only been allowed to recite the poem,

probably she would be content to *phweet* the whistle. But now things were different. Now, if she didn't do anything about it, the entire day would go by and she would never be noticed. She would be a nothing. She would be a nonparticipant, a bystander, a nonentity, a nerd.

A month from now, back in Stuttgart or Brussels or Liverpool, or wherever, the educators would remember their visit to American schools, and they would think of—

Yuck. Jacob Berman. They would think, "That wonderful intelligent boy in a junior high school in a Boston suburb; that boy who quoted long passages from Sophocles, imagine that . . ."

And they would think of—

Barf. Emily Ewing. They would think, "That stunning girl with the perfect teeth and the smooth, shiny, long hair; too bad she didn't know much about poetry, but even so . . ."

But if someone, by chance, asked, "What about Anastasia Krupnik?" they would scratch their heads. They would furrow their brows. They would say, finally,

"WHO?"

Anastasia couldn't bear it. The worst thing in the world, she decided, was to be on the receiving end of a brow-furrowed WHO.

So she decided to disrupt the gym class. And she hoped that she could do it in a way that would make Ms. Wilhelmina Willoughby proud.

It was a different group of visitors in the gym, Anastasia noticed as she marched in with her classmates, all of them in their clean, starched gym suits, white socks, and newly washed white sneakers.

Jenny Billings had tried to get away with forgetting the white socks. "I'm sorry, Ms. Willoughby," Jenny Billings had said smugly in the locker room, "but I forgot my white socks. So I guess I'll just have to wear these striped knee socks."

"No way, José," Ms. Willoughby replied. "Be my guest, kiddo." And she held up a brand-new pair of white socks from the supply she had waiting. Jenny groaned, took the fresh socks, and went to change.

Anastasia glanced over at the guests, who were seated in a row in the bleachers, as she stood in her place in the lines of seventh-grade girls. Ms. Willoughby was making a little speech about the kinds of things they'd been doing in gym.

As usual, the educators were taking notes. This group included two Japanese—or maybe Chinese, Anastasia wasn't sure—gentlemen and a tall black woman in robes from some African country. There was also a woman in an Indian sari, with one long braid down her back and a red spot on her forehead.

Standing there with her legs—the skinniest legs in the entire world, she was quite certain—exposed, feeling half-naked and very unattractive, Anastasia wondered if the kids in those countries had to wear stupid-looking blue gym suits in their schools. She watched the foreigners writing diligently in their little notebooks.

"Tall girl with glasses at end of row six," she was sure they were writing. "Only girl in class wearing whistle on cord around neck. Skinniest legs in the world. Very awkward-looking. Probably will be unable to climb rope."

Hah. Wait till I show them. All of them, even Ms. Wilhelmina Willoughby.

"Now"—Ms. Willoughby was concluding her

speech—"I'm going to have this group of girls demonstrate rope-climbing. Anastasia Krupnik, there at the end of row six, has very kindly volunteered to direct the exercise. Anastasia, would you step forward?"

Anastasia felt a new surge of love for Ms. Willoughby, who had done her absolute most tactful best to make it sound as if she had been specially selected as director, rather than the truth: that she had to blow the whistle because she had never been able to do better than dangle eighteen inches off the ground.

Ms. Willoughby would be truly pleased by the surprise, Anastasia decided.

She stepped forward to the spot that Ms. Willoughby indicated; Ms. Willoughby went over to the bleachers and sat down with the row of attentive educators.

Phweet! Anastasia blew the whistle, and the first six girls moved forward to the ropes and began to climb.

Watching, it suddenly occurred to Anastasia that rope-climbing was, after all, a pretty dumb exercise. How often would you need to climb a rope in real life? How many of the girls in this class would become mountain climbers? How many would need to escape from prison? (Daphne, maybe, if she didn't outgrow her adolescent pranks.) How many would have to be rescued from a rooftop by a helicopter? How many would—

Thump, thump, thump, thump, thump, thump. One by one, Sonya, Jenny, Erin, Edith, Marie, and Jill dropped from the ends of the ropes to the mats that were spread on the floor, and went back to their places.

Ho hum. *Phweet.* It sure wasn't very exciting being the whistle-blower. But at least, Anastasia thought, her classmates were doing the rope-climbing quickly, so the period wouldn't end before her moment of glory.

She watched, trying to look interested and attentive, as Karen, Daphne, Melissa, Liz, and the Wilcox twins climbed the ropes.

Thump, thump, thump, thump, thump, thump.
Phweet. And the third row of six girls climbed.

Anastasia began taking some deep breaths. She wasn't actually *nervous,* she decided, but maybe a little apprehensive. After all, she had only climbed the rope in her garage once. And it wasn't as high as the ropes in the gym.

Thump, thump, thump, thump, thump, thump.

Phweet. The last row of girls—only four in this final group—went to the ropes. Meredith, Jessica, Bonnie, and Mary Ellen began to climb.

Anastasia glanced at the educators to be certain they were paying attention. One of the Japanese men was looking at his watch, but she decided that didn't mean he was bored. He was probably just admiring his watch, since it was probably made in Japan; Anastasia's father's watch was made in Japan, and it did so many digital things that Dr. Krupnik said he was surprised it didn't write haiku as well.

Thump. Meredith landed on the mat.

Thump. Bonnie landed.

Thump, thump. Jessica and Mary Ellen eased themselves down from the ropes, and the four girls went back to the waiting lines.

Anastasia saw Ms. Willoughby rise from her seat in the bleachers and start forward. Well, it was now or never; she knew Ms. Willoughby was about to say thank you to the girls and to the visitors, and then everyone would be dismissed.

PHWEET! Anastasia blew very hard on the whistle. Ms. Willoughby looked startled. The lady in the sari jumped slightly in her seat. All twenty-two girls in their gym suits stared at Anastasia to see what was going on. Daphne formed the words "Go for it!" silently with her mouth.

Anastasia stepped forward and faced the small audience on the bleachers. Ms. Willoughby was starting to sit down, starting to stand up again, and finally sitting back down, puzzled.

"Ah," Anastasia began, "there's going to be one final brief demonstration, and it will be me."

No one was taking notes. But their hands, with pens in them, were all poised over their notebooks.

"I want to explain," Anastasia went on, "that the reason I was only blowing the whistle was because I couldn't seem to climb a rope.

"I tried and tried but all I could do was dangle because I couldn't get the feet part right, and then my arms would start to hurt.

"And, ah, Ms. Wilhelmina Willoughby, the gym teacher sitting there on your right—well, she kept encouraging me so that I began to practice a lot at home. She told me that one day I'd just keep right on going up the rope to the top. And I didn't really believe her, I guess, but I kept trying, and, ah, well . . ."

She stopped. She couldn't think what else to say. "Well, you watch," she said, finally. "I'll show you."

Anastasia turned and went to the closest rope. Suddenly she remembered the one final thing she had intended to say.

"I owe it all to my gym teacher, Ms. Wilhelmina Willoughby," she said. Then she leaped and grabbed the rope as high as she could.

For a moment she dangled, the way she always had. But carefully she felt for the rope with her legs and feet, remembering how, last night in the garage, everything had come together for her.

There. There it was—the rope, in the correct position, and her sneakers grasping it just right. The feeling came back, the same feeling of power and control she had had last night, and she knew she would make it.

Up. She hauled herself with her arms, and felt herself rise along the rope. Up farther. Her feet grasped again, and the muscles in her legs pushed.

Up some more. Now her hands were more certain, and her legs moved just the right way, and she went faster.

Up and up. She had passed, now, the height of her

garage rope, she knew. But she still had a distance to go, and she was sure now that she could make it. Below her, she could hear her classmates murmur. For them, it had been nothing, this trip up a rope — but each of them had seen Anastasia fail at it again and again.

Her glasses shifted on her nose and she realized that she was sweating a bit. It didn't matter. She didn't need to see. All she needed was the feel of the thick rope in her newly confident hands and then the feel of the knot in the upper end which would tell her she had made it to the top.

There: there it was, the knot. She was at the very top of the rope, the place she had thought she could never, ever achieve. Ms. Wilhelmina Willoughby had been absolutely right when she had said, "One of these days, Anastasia, you'll amaze yourself."

I have, Anastasia thought. I've amazed myself. A week ago I thought I could never in a million years get to this spot, and now here I am: in front of a whole audience. I did it! This is the happiest moment of my life. And I'm just as glad that there wasn't time for me to say my poem in English class, because *this* is the absolutely right time for that poem, and won't they all be truly astounded now, because here goes:

"'O world!'" Anastasia exclaimed. "'I cannot hold thee close enough!'"

Sure enough, it was just as Mr. Rafferty had predicted. Suddenly, now that she was overcome with emotion, the gestures came naturally. Anastasia flung out her arms.

And fell.

Who What When Where Why

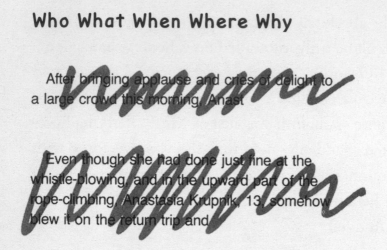

After bringing applause and cries of delight to a large crowd this morning, Anast

Even though she had done just fine at the whistle-blowing, and in the upward part of the rope-climbing, Anastasia Krupnik, 13, somehow blew it on the return trip and

This morning, in front of twenty-two girls in royal blue gym suits and white socks, and a batch of visiting international educators sitting in the bleachers along with Ms. Wilhelmina Willoughby, Anastasia Krupnik, 13, plummeted from the top of the junior high gym and never got to finish the poem she was reciting.

twelve

Anastasia opened her eyes and saw a ceiling that she was quite certain she had never seen before. Not wanting to move her head, which hurt a surprising amount for just one head, she slid her eyes first to the left and then to the right.

On one side she saw an unfamiliar table and an unfamiliar wall calendar. On the other side she saw an unfamiliar window with unfamiliar curtains, and through the window, she saw a tiny bit of an unfamiliar tree.

She was, she realized, in a bed—an unfamiliar bed. At the foot of the bed she saw a woman—an unfamiliar woman with gray-streaked hair—standing and looking at her.

Oh, great, Anastasia said to herself. I'm going to have to say the worst line of dialogue ever. Might as well get it over with.

She sighed. "Where am I?" she asked.

The woman moved forward, smiling. "Hi," she said. "You're in the hospital. I'm Dr. McCartin."

The doctor leaned more closely over Anastasia and looked into her eyes with an instrument. Anastasia could smell her perfume.

"Do you remember what happened?" Dr. McCartin asked, after she stood back up.

Anastasia frowned. She did remember, sort of. First she had been in English class, listening to el nerdo Jacob Berman; then she had gone to gym—oh, yes, *gym;* that was it. She had blown the whistle—just thinking about it made her headache worse—and then she had made that stupid speech, and then she had . . .

Had she? Or was she just imagining it?

"I climbed the rope in gym, I think," she said tentatively to the doctor.

"Good!" the doctor replied.

"What do you mean, good? It was *great!*" Anastasia said. "Do you realize I'd been trying for *months* to climb that rope?" She began to pull herself up, and then stopped. "*Ouch*. My head really hurts," she complained.

The doctor was pumping up a blood pressure cuff on Anastasia's right arm. "Shhh," she said. "Lie back."

Anastasia eased herself back onto the pillow. I *fell*, she thought suddenly. I must have fallen from that rope.

She remembered the time that Sam had fallen, last summer, from his bedroom window, and had been taken by ambulance to the hospital. Now here she had gone and done practically the same thing, she realized. How stupid can you get? And my parents are probably all worried, the way they were then, when Sam had the fractured skull and had to have an operation and had to—

"Oh, NO!" Anastasia yelped suddenly.

The doctor popped the stethoscope out of her ears and looked at her quizzically. "What's the matter?" she asked. "Besides a headache, of course."

I'm going to be a good sport, Anastasia thought.

I'll be mature. I won't cry. I'll learn to wear a turban or something.

"You had to shave my hair off, didn't you?" she wailed.

Dr. McCartin looked startled. "Good heavens, no," she said. "You only have a concussion. I'm going to send you home in a couple of hours, I think, if you promise not to climb any ropes for a few days."

Anastasia groaned.

"Want to try sitting up? There are a lot of people waiting out in the lounge to see you. Shall I let them come in?"

Dr. McCartin cranked up the head of the bed slowly. Anastasia felt dizzy for a moment, but then the dizziness faded. Her headache throbbed a bit, but it wasn't unbearable. Carefully she felt her head with her hand. There was a bump, and some soreness, but her hair was still there, thank goodness.

"Sure," Anastasia said, feeling a little like royalty, "allow them to come in."

Anastasia looked around the hospital room from where she sat in the position of honor in her bed. It was astounding. Never before in her entire thirteen years had so many people gathered just to pay attention to her.

There were her parents, of course, right beside the bed, still looking a little worried. "Honest," Anastasia kept reassuring them, "I'm *fine*."

There was Sam, sitting on Gertrude Stein's lap. Sam had been smuggled in because he was too young, technically, to visit in the hospital. "If you had bashed your head harder," Sam said, "you would have been a baldy, like I was."

"True," Anastasia acknowledged.

"And harder than *that*," Sam added, "and you would have been *dead*."

"Well, Sam, I don't think—"

"We could have had a funeral," Sam said sweetly, "and buried you in the earth like little birds and bugs and animals and Aunt Rose."

"*Sam*," whispered Anastasia, "*shhh*." She glanced nervously toward Uncle George to see if he had heard. But Uncle George was over in the corner of the room, talking very pleasantly to—was that right? Was she seeing correctly? Anastasia sat up farther in the bed and peered beyond her father's shoulder.

Sure enough. It was Daphne's mother, smiling

pleasantly and talking with animation to Uncle George. And there was Daphne, grinning at Anastasia.

"Did I disrupt gym class or did I not disrupt gym class?" Anastasia asked her.

"For sure," Daphne answered, rolling her eyes. "You should have seen everybody rushing around calling ambulances and stuff. And guess who was absolutely the most worried person there."

"That nervous-looking Japanese guy who kept checking his watch?"

"Shhh," whispered Daphne. "That guy's right over there in the corner of the room. It wasn't him anyway. It was— Well, here, I'll let her tell you."

Daphne stepped aside to let Ms. Wilhelmina Willoughby approach the bed. She didn't even have a layered-look outfit on; she had just thrown a trench coat over her shorts and sweatshirt.

"Anastasia, you were amazing," Ms. Willoughby said. "*Amazing*."

"I climbed the rope okay, didn't I? The only reason I fell," Anastasia said, "was—"

"I know. Because you threw your arms out. Your rope-climbing was perfect. A-plus for rope-climbing.

But why on earth did you throw your arms out that way at the top?"

Gingerly, Anastasia shook her head. "It's too complicated to explain, Ms. Willoughby."

"Well," her gym teacher said, "you certainly scared everyone to death, most of all *me*. But you're okay, that's the important thing. And I've had a chance to meet your family: your nice parents, and your brother, and your very charming uncle from California—"

Uncle George and Ms. Wilhelmina Willoughby? Suddenly Anastasia remembered what Daphne had told her just a few days before: that Ms. Wilhelmina Willoughby had no man in her life. Hmmmmm. How did "Aunt Wilhelmina" sound? Not too bad. Anastasia glanced around to see if Uncle George was still totally involved with Daphne's mother. But no; Daphne's mother was now talking to the lady in the Indian sari—my goodness, that whole group of international educators was in the hospital room too!

And there was Uncle George, off in a different corner now, talking to Dr. McCartin, who—Anastasia took a closer look at her doctor. Hmmmm. She was actually a pretty attractive lady, once she got that stethoscope out of her ears. Anastasia wondered if she was married, and decided that she would have to find a tactful way to ask. Of course there was no rush. It was still a little soon — just over a week since Aunt Rose's death — for Uncle George to remarry.

She felt exhausted. It had, after all, been an eventful day. Anastasia leaned back on the pillows and looked around the room filled with people.

Her parents looked more relaxed now that Anastasia had been talking cheerfully and sitting up comfortably in the bed. She had the greatest parents in the world, Anastasia decided, even if neither of them had much fashion sense (her mother was wearing jeans and a paint-smeared shirt, as usual; her father was wearing incredibly hideous baggy pants that he had bought probably in 1960).

Sam had leaned back in Mrs. Stein's lap and was sucking his fingers dreamily. Probably, Anastasia thought, he was planning another funeral. She was going to have to have a very serious talk with old Sam when her head stopped aching. Maybe she could help him find a new hobby. She really loved Sam a lot, and an older sister owed it to a little brother to try to guide him through life.

Gertrude Stein looked as if she had found Perfect Happiness, holding Sam on her lap. She had never had any children of her own. It was the luckiest thing for her, *and* for us, Anastasia thought, when we moved into the house next door. We got a brand-new grandmother and she got a brand-new family. Maybe I shouldn't try so hard to find her a man friend—especially a glamorous one—because he might whisk her away to live in Las Vegas or something.

Glamorous Uncle George was still talking to the doctor. They both looked very serious, and Anastasia thought he was probably telling her about how Aunt Rose had gotten zapped by a swordfish steak, compliments of Sal Monella. Poor Aunt Rose. Poor Uncle George. Anastasia felt sorry for everybody who had lost somebody . . .

Except Mrs. Bellingham, she realized suddenly. Daphne's mother, who so very recently had been grouchy and depressed, was apparently recovering. She had a new, becoming haircut; she was wearing eye makeup, something Anastasia had never seen on Caroline Bellingham before, certainly not when she was married to the Reverend Bellingham; and she was talking vivaciously to several of the international educators. One of the Japanese men was writing something on a small piece of paper—maybe Mrs. Bellingham's phone number? I wonder, thought Anastasia, what Daphne would think if . . .

Her eyes found Daphne's across the room. Daphne shrugged, grinned, and winked. Her blond Shirley Temple curls glistened, and Anastasia realized that Daphne would be a real big hit in Tokyo or Yokohama—or *anywhere,* for that matter. Daphne would be okay. Daphne had class.

Finally, Anastasia glanced over at Ms. Wilhelmina Willoughby. Talk about class! Even in her trench coat, Ms. Wilhelmina Willoughby looked as if she should be on the cover of *Vogue.* More than that, though, the bright sparkle in her eyes and the graceful way she moved, now, as she turned to leave, stopping in the doorway to wave affectionately to Anastasia—well, no question; on a scale of one to ten, Ms. Wilhelmina Willoughby was definitely a ten, and Anastasia didn't care who knew she felt that way. Maybe she *did* have a crush on her gym teacher. So what? Her mother thought it was okay. It *felt* okay. And Ms. Wilhelmina Willoughby didn't seem to mind.

Watching the room full of people as they began, now, to gather their belongings in order to leave, Anastasia tried in her mind to create a newspaper story. Who? she asked herself.

Mom, Dad, Sam, Gertrude Stein, Uncle George, Daphne, Mrs. Bellingham, Dr. McCartin, Ms. Wilhelmina Willoughby, and six international educators—

What?

Had gathered together around the bed of Anastasia Krupnik—

When?

Anastasia wasn't at all sure. Probably it was Wednesday still, she decided—

Where?

In a small hospital room—

Why?

Because— Anastasia hesitated. Then she realized what the truth was. They all think I'm pretty special, Anastasia told herself, and she hoped that it didn't count as conceited if she didn't say it aloud.

More great books by *Lois Lowry!*

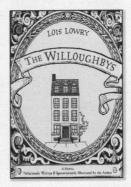

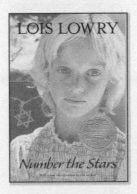

A Newbery Medal Winner

*Award-winning fiction from **Karen Cushman!***

A Newbery Medal Winner

Newbery Honor Book

The best of *Mary Downing Hahn!*

**Winner of the Scott O'Dell
Book Award**

The Lemonade War Series

When life gives you lemons, make lemonade!

Looking for more great fiction? Then check these out!